D1430034

HOW TO NOT SUCK AT LIFE

89 TIPS
FOR TEENS

Connor Boyack

LIBERTAS PRESS

Copyright © 2021 by Connor Boyack.

All rights reserved. No part of this publication may be reproduced, distributed or transmitted in any form or by any means, including photocopying, recording, or other electronic or mechanical methods, without the prior written permission of the publisher.

Libertas Press
2183 West Main, Ste. A102
Lehi, UT 84043

How to Not Suck at Life: 89 Tips for Teens — 1st ed.

ISBN-13 978-1-943521-76-0 (paperback)

For bulk orders, send inquiries to info@libertas.org.

10 9 8 7 6 5 4 3 2 1

CONTENTS

INTRODUCTION

I WAS A LATE bloomer. Even worse, I was in marching band in high school.

Put those two together, and you have a really awkward group photo. There we were, dressed up in our outfits, lined up by height so the tall people could be sorted in the back of the photo, while rows of shorter people filed in toward the front. As the last of the line approached the group to be placed in position, I counted over 15 girls ahead of me in line. Only two girls were shorter than me. It was, as I said, awkward.

Puberty later set in, obviously, and boy was I grateful. But it had nothing to do with me; I didn't put in any effort on my part. These physical changes we all go through were a natural development that happened to me.

What about my mental development? More importantly, what about yours?

Unlike our bodies, our minds won't just magically learn what they need to; our attitudes, behaviors, values, and opinions are things we learn and control ourselves. They change over time and are influenced by all kinds of factors. The problem is that many people treat their minds as passively as they do their bodies; they're acted upon instead of acting of their own accord. They go with the flow, content to just do what others do and think what others think. They're lemmings, following the crowd.

But you don't want to just do what others think you should do. You're an individual. You want to be careful about what you think and do. You know that the mind is a powerful thing and that we need to learn how to use it well so that we're happy and successful in life. So here you are, reading this book. If you're ready, it's time to consider some unconventional ideas and powerful ways of thinking that will help you level up in life. Ready to get started?

DON'T FOLLOW THE POPULAR PATH

A FEW YEARS AGO, an unsuspecting woman arrived at an eye clinic after seeing an advertisement for a free exam. She checked in and took a seat in the reception area, surrounded by a handful of people. While perusing one of the available magazines, she was startled by a loud beep from the overhead speaker. Suddenly, everyone seated nearby stood up, then promptly sat back down. The woman's weirded-out glance revealed her discomfort with the situation... what was going on?

After the process repeated itself several times, the woman began acting the same as the others. Without having any clue as to what was going on, she stood up next time the beep sounded—then again, and again. For minutes, the beep prompted everyone to stand up and sit down. But then it got weirder. One by one, the other people were called into the doctor's office, ultimately leaving only the woman in the reception area. All alone, she continued to stand up for the beep, having no idea why.

As it turns out, this was an experiment set up by the TV show *Brain Games* on the *National*

Geographic channel. Everyone was in on it except the woman; the people sitting nearby were all actors. It was a simple demonstration of social conditioning, showing how people are persuaded by what others do. There are countless real-world examples, of course, from people buying toilet paper during the early part of the COVID-19 pandemic just because everyone else was, to believing something that's actually "fake news" simply because it went viral. People tend to believe or do what's popular among the crowd, even if there's no reason for it.

This is called having a "herd mentality" and it's extremely common among teenagers (and many adults never grow out of it). But what's popular and what's right are often two different things. So, when the masses are mindlessly moving from one popular trend to the next or simply believing what they're told by people in authority, that's the perfect time for you to hit the pause button and consider whether it's the right thing for you to do. Don't just assume that what everyone else thinks or does is what you should think or do. Chances are, they're wrong.

GET AN APPRENTICESHIP, OR FIVE

I RECENTLY TOOK MY kids to a new ice cream store for a treat. We had never been to this place, and they had a wide range of options with clever nicknames and odd combinations of ingredients. I had a bit of "decision paralysis." I had so many options that I didn't know what to do. But I snapped out of it when one of the employees offered to give me a sample of anything I wanted.

This was a super helpful offer, since the flavor I thought I would like ended up being not that great. I sampled a few options and then made a smarter decision. I was happy with the outcome because I didn't waste my money on something I would regret.

Likewise, the world offers you many options for what you can spend your life doing. There are tens of thousands of types of jobs (or more), and even crazier, most of the jobs that will be available in your adulthood don't even exist yet. Technology has a way of changing things.

So, before you commit your life to a particular path, do what I did at the ice cream shop: sample the selections before making any big decisions. There are various ways to do this. One option is a formal apprenticeship where you can learn a particular trade or task under the guidance of an expert. You offer to work for free (or are sometimes paid) and learn on the job, much like an internship (the key difference being that an apprenticeship is longer in duration and typically involves more structure and mentorship). Or it can be even easier and informal; simply "job shadow" people who work in professions that intrigue you. Get your parents to help network and find people who are carpenters or lawyers or botanists or mechanics... whatever interests you, then ask if you can follow them around for a few days and ask questions. You'll get a sneak peek into whether they enjoy their job, what it's actually like, and whether you want to commit a large portion of your life to it.

Many people commit large amounts of time and money to pursuing a career they end up not liking. Don't be like them; sample the selection before deciding.

DITCH THE EGO

NEWS FLASH: THE WORLD doesn't revolve around you.

I remember others (mostly my parents) telling me this during my teen years. But as a teenager, it's sometimes hard to process this accusation because prideful people rarely think they're prideful.

In reality, many teenagers (and, sadly, adults) do things that disregard the feelings and interests of others. They focus on themselves and think that things ought to be done on their timeline, the way they want. They don't focus on or care much about the preferences of others; they're unlikely to sacrifice their desires to, instead, do what someone else prefers.

As the saying goes, "There are two kinds of days for teenagers: good days, and days when things don't go their way." But this saying isn't written in stone, and it doesn't need to be a description of your behavior. To some extent, you're not to blame for this tendency. The rational part of the adolescent brain (the "prefrontal cortex," if you want to Google it) is still developing, and your body is being bathed in hormones that create impulses and moods that are difficult to manage. But adults who've outgrown these pubescent phases still can be egocentric monsters. You'd be wise to try to restrain this behavior early on so you can become a helpful, positive person whom others want to be around and support. It'll be good for your personal and professional relationships, and an early effort now will pay dividends down the road.

Not a fan of the restaurant your parents picked? Don't complain and insist on going somewhere you like; go along to get along. Prefer to watch a different movie than what others picked? Hold back your opinion and be willing to do what others decide. Resist the urge to speak your mind on every topic that's discussed or to vocalize what you think is stupid or wrong. It's not always about you. In short, be a decent person who cares about the opinions and interests of those around you, and, in the short and long term, you'll enjoy life more and be happier.

PUT COMPOUND INTEREST TO WORK

TEENAGERS OFTEN LIKE TO be lazy, so why not apply this to your financial future? From a young age, I had a mutual fund where my money would grow on autopilot, without any effort on my part. But the magic really happens over the long term. Let's use a specific example to illustrate.

Imagine you have $500 in savings at age 16. If you put this in a Roth IRA or other investment account and earned around 5% interest that year from that investment, by the end of that year, you would have $525, an increase of $25. But for that next year, you now have $525 invested, so 5% on that total amount would be $551.25, an increase of $26.25. And as the interest gets invested along with your original amount (the "principal"), the amount continues increasing each year.

Fast forward to your 50s. That original $500 you put in, without any additional money saved, would become a whopping $2,727 by the time you're 50. Imagine, instead, that you invested $50 a month at this 5% rate, starting when you were 16. By the time you were 50, you would have invested $20,400 of your own money, which would have turned into a total of $53,455. Of course, as you get older and earn more, you can put even larger amounts in—say, $10% of all your income—and then generate even more interest, which would then create even more gains in the future.

Even if you started with nothing at age 18 and began putting in $300 per month at a 5% rate, your $115,200 of contributions would turn into $283,434 by age 50. But 5% might be too conservative; it's possible to get 10% interest. At that rate, you would have $835,537, nearly three times higher.

The point of all this? Compound interest basically helps you earn free money. Plan wisely with your parents now, and you could easily be a millionaire by the time you retire. Set aside a portion of your earnings and let compound interest go to work for you.

QUESTION EVERYTHING...
OR MOST THINGS

THE WORLD WAS SHOCKED in 1990 as a young Kuwaiti woman, Nayirah, testified through tears before the Congressional Human Rights Caucus regarding crimes committed by Iraqi soldiers. She claimed that soldiers took babies out of incubators in a Kuwaiti hospital and left them to die. Representatives, Senators, and the President of the United States cited Nayirah's testimony as they advocated for war against Iraq. Americans were shocked and outraged at the allegations being made, for they were disgusting and cruel.

They were also false.

Only later was it discovered that Nayirah was the daughter of the Kuwaiti ambassador to the United States, and that she had been coached by an advertising agency that was paid millions of dollars by Citizens for a Free Kuwait, a public relations committee created by officials at the Kuwaiti embassy. As one reporter wrote, "The incubator story seriously distorted the American debate about whether to support military action." But that was the point; the advertising agency had spent a million dollars provided by the Kuwaiti royal family to determine how best to sway American public opinion.

People often lie, and people in power, even more so. It's essential that you be critical of others; healthy skepticism will help you avoid being suckered into believing or doing something that's wrong. Even well-intentioned people pass on ideas that turn out to be misguided or incorrect, and this includes authority figures like doctors, church leaders, politicians, and even, perhaps, your parents! You want to know the truth, and that requires sometimes un-learning what you previously accepted to be true. It is not wrong to analyze your opinions and beliefs and see if they withstand scrutiny; the status quo isn't inherently right. Indeed, in many cases, you'll come to see that what you were taught was true, but because you investigated and challenged it, you'll understand that truth more deeply and be better able to defend it.

The world is full of manipulators, deceives, or well-intentioned ignoramuses spreading their confusion as fact. Avoid their traps and question what they say.

LEARN HOW TO LEARN

ON JUNE 25, 2010, 18-year-old Erica Goldson stood at a podium in front of her peers and their parents. Behind her sat the administrators and teachers of the school from which she was graduating. As school valedictorian, Erica now had the opportunity to speak to her graduating class. To say that Erica's words were unexpected would be a tremendous understatement.

"I cannot say that I am any more intelligent than my peers," Erica announced. "I can attest that I am only the best at doing what I am told and working the system."

She continued: "Yet, here I stand, and I am supposed to be proud that I have completed this period of indoctrination. I will leave in the fall to go on to the next phase expected of me, in order to receive a paper document that certifies that I am capable of work. A worker is someone who is trapped within repetition, a slave of the system set up before him. But now, I have successfully shown that I was the best slave. I did what I was told to the extreme."

Erica went on to explain that she focused on memorizing what she was told and performing well on tests. She felt lost: "I have no interests because I saw every subject of study as work, and I excelled at every subject just for the purpose of excelling, not learning." The school system failed Erica because she was told *what* to learn, not *how* to learn. She was not given the time or freedom to focus on learning what interested her.

This failure is one that you can avoid, whether you're in public school or not. And honestly, what you learn in your youth will usually be irrelevant to your later life, anyway. Memorizing facts and formulas should be less important to you than learning how to learn, developing an ability to gain and retain new information easily. For starters, watch Barbara Oakley's *Learning How to Learn* video on YouTube, or get her book for teens (it has the same title).

THE COOL KIDS
SOON WON'T BE

THERE'S A CASTE SYSTEM of sorts that develops in high school. Cliques are created in which the cool kids are well known to everyone else and set themselves up as influencers of the inferior rest of their peers. When this is the only world you know, it seems like the popular kids hold a lot of sway. You might feel tempted to be like them and have them like you. The closer you are to them, the more your own social status would increase.

But here's the thing: one's popularity as a teenager is no indication of one's success as an adult. Quite often, the nerdiest introverts become the tech megastars, wealthy business owners, and praised leaders envied by the masses, a huge contrast to their earlier life. And the popular kids in high school often fade into obscurity, some trying to cling to their glory days by resisting moving on with their lives.

Here's an experiment: have your parents do some social media research to track down the "cool kids" from their youth and see what their lives are like. Ask your relatives or your friends' parents to do the same. Granted, there are always exceptions; this isn't a hard-and-fast rule. But quite often, they will have made choices that produced a life not worth emulating, certainly one that's no longer "cool."

The lesson? Life is distorted as a teenager. What seems popular now soon won't be. Those you want to emulate today will tomorrow become forgettable. Your preferences will change, as will your perceptions about what type of behavior you want to emulate. Forget what's popular or cool and focus on developing your talents and education to set yourself up for future success. Fads change, as will you. Count on it, and plan accordingly.

TAKE RISKS

YOUR PARENTS OR GRANDPARENTS are at a point in life when doing something risky is likely out of the question because they have bills, obligations, children, and responsibilities that depend on predictability and stability. Moving the path they've established can cause chaos... if they made a financially risky decision, it could ruin their retirement or bankrupt them. That's not very wise.

But that doesn't apply to you. You're young and largely free of responsibilities. You don't have debt, children, or other obligations that weigh on you. You're able to be nimble and flexible. You can take risks; and that window of opportunity will only exist for another handful of years.

Jeff Bezos, founder of Amazon.com, is one of the richest people in the world. He left a comfortable, high-paying job to start up his new company, and the risks were high. Why did he make the leap? "I had to project myself forward to age 80," he explained. "I don't want to be 80 years old, cataloging a bunch of major regrets of my life." You see, countless adults do catalog these regrets. They never tried their hand at entrepreneurship, never pursued that hobby, never asked that one person out, never traveled alone, never moved somewhere new. Many people choose safety and comfort over what's new and unknown. And that's understandable, of course; stability is familiar, and something unknown might become a problem.

But those problems are smaller when you're younger. You don't have a large fortune to lose. You don't have only a few years of life left to pivot if you fail. You won't be risking the safety of a spouse or children as well. So, take advantage of your youth to pursue success seriously. You won't achieve your dreams by playing it safe; inaction leads nowhere.

Take some time to think through what this means for you. What would be a bold move? Moving to a new location that has better job opportunities? Starting your own business? Skipping college to pursue something else? Taking a year off to travel and experience other cultures? Whatever it is, recognize that the safest time to make risky decisions is when you're young, and the results can help grow your self-esteem while generating new possibilities in your life that wouldn't have previously been possible. Just make sure to look before you leap.

DON'T TAKE IT PERSONALLY

I WAS A LATE bloomer, which means that I was a target for being picked on during most of my high school years. I was pushed around, picked up and put into garbage cans, and called all kinds of names. I took it personally. I thought these bullies hated me, so I began to hate myself.

That was a mistake. These attacks had nothing to do with me and everything to do with the people doing them. These predators had their own problems they were dealing with and decided to take it out on me to compensate for their own insecurities and issues. They tried to make themselves feel better by making someone else feel worse.

We all hate when someone cuts in line in front of us, but that person doesn't want to cut us; they just want to get to the front. The person who criticizes something we believe in isn't trying to call us an idiot; they're attacking an idea. In so many cases, people's motives are different than what we might suspect them to be. And when we get emotional, thinking that it's about us, we waste all kinds of time and energy that could be better put to use.

Even when someone seems to attack you directly, it's worth it to calmly consider what might have prompted the person to act that way. Perhaps they misinterpreted something you did, leading them to think their attack was justified? Maybe the person has some mental health problems or physical pain that's provoking a bad temper or mood disorder. It could even be something upstream in their life like childhood abuse or their parents going through a nasty divorce.

Be careful about making assumptions about others' intentions because, even when someone does something against you "on purpose," there may be an explanation for it or many influences in that person's life that give context for why they behaved that way. Look for the bigger picture and realize that their behavior is more about them than about you.

YOUR ENEMY MIGHT BE YOUR FRIEND

IN MY MID-20S, I made a good number of enemies. I was vocal about telling people when I thought their opinions were wrong, and naturally, those people didn't take lightly to some kid arguing publicly that they were misguided. It wasn't a good start to my budding political career.

A few years later, I came to realize that fighting individuals was wrong; I should have been fighting ideas. By focusing on policies instead of people, I could separate a person from their opinions and still keep a relationship with someone even without being a fan of what they did or believed. This realization came largely because I found myself on the same side as people whom I had a poor relationship with, and it was... awkward.

In my line of work, I have to interact with elected officials, some of whom were previously my enemies whom I would lambast when they did something I thought wrong. To this day, they remember my behavior, as do I, and it continues to complicate our relationship. But now, I've learned that with any given elected official, I might disagree strongly with 20% of what they vote for or believe in, yet on the rest of the issues, they could be one of my greatest champions to push forward something we both believe is right.

In my younger years, I didn't value relationships or realize the long-term consequences of my interactions with people. I came to later see that I needed to compartmentalize a bit and not treat a person poorly just because I disagreed with them on one thing. Sometimes, that person would change their opinion, or I would change mine. Life has a way of bringing things full circle, and your former "enemies" might later become your best allies. So, take the long view and recognize that the person you currently love to hate might one day be the person you hate to have to love.

TAKE RESPONSIBILITY FOR YOUR ACTIONS

EVERY YEAR, OUR ORGANIZATION runs a series of children's markets for kids to sell things to the public. It's a ton of fun and always well attended. A couple years ago, I was at a gas station when the woman in the car next to me recognized me and said that she had participated with her kids in the recent market. I was happy to hear that and smiled, but she then quickly chewed me out.

Her children apparently sold nothing, and, therefore, they "wasted" the $10 booth fee. She was upset with me that her children, who were all in the car and could hear this conversation, didn't succeed. She said I should have had more people in attendance and made several other suggestions.

Here's the real reason why her kids didn't succeed: this mother bought some store-brand chips and sodas, sat her kids in front of the table, and expected people to buy the marked-up, boring items when there were homemade cinnamon rolls, freshly spun cotton candy, and other items at booths nearby. She didn't put in any effort on behalf of her children, but she refused to take responsibility. She was playing the victim and blaming me for her problems.

This was foolish and deprived her children of a great learning opportunity to understand what went wrong and how to correct it. This "blame game" is extremely common, certainly among teenagers, but even among adults. It's easy to avoid accountability by shifting the reason for failure to someone else. It may be tempting to do. However, doing so prevents growth and cultivates a victimhood mindset in which your problems are the fault of someone else.

But they're not. You can overcome your problems. You can acknowledge your mistakes and move past them. By refusing to blame other people when things go poorly, you can hold yourself accountable for any mistakes or bad behavior, and actually improve, becoming a more productive and positive person all around. This is the way.

SKIP COLLEGE

FOR DECADES THERE HAS been an invisible conveyor belt shepherding young students through their schooling experience. I was on it, along with all my peers, without realizing it. In high school, I was preparing for college; it was simply what you did. I was never encouraged to question that process; it was assumed to be *the* process.

But that's changing. A recent survey of 600 human resource leaders, those responsible for hiring people for their companies, large and small, found that "90 percent were open to hiring a candidate without a four-year degree." That's a staggering statistic and one that undermines the long-held notion that going to college is a prerequisite to getting a good job. As one HR manager said, "Our education system is not keeping up with the needs businesses have, and what is most important today should be proof of skills and the ability to deliver results." Forty-seven percent of these HR leaders felt that colleges aren't preparing students for the real world; yet the conveyor belt steadily moves in the same direction, with hordes of humans being herded through college.

It wasn't until years after I graduated from college that I began to really question its purpose. What milestones in life could I have achieved had I not spent four more years at a school desk? What career advancements might I have reached if I had a head start? These and more questions became all the more tantalizing as I began seeing more and more stories about successful college dropouts and entrepreneurs who never attended at all.

There is value, educational, social, and professional, to being on a campus and obtaining a degree. And, to be sure, certain professions absolutely require that you obtain a college credential. But the overall benefits of attending college have to be weighed against their alternatives. And with each passing day, there are more alternatives that allow you to become educated and successful without the wasted time and money of pursuing a college degree. Search them out and consider if they are right for you. Read my book, *Skip College*, for some ideas.

READ WIDELY AND OFTEN

ONE IN FOUR AMERICANS hasn't read a book in the last year in any form: print, electronic, or audiobooks. Overall, Americans spend just 17 minutes a day reading something that they aren't required to for work or school. On the other hand, Americans spend over 13 hours each day consuming media via their TV, computer, tablet, or phone.

Of course, you can learn a lot from reading digital content, but there's so much garbage online that people pass for "news." Many feel informed only with superficial sound bites and infotainment that doesn't provide intellectual substance; it doesn't enrich people's lives or edify them to become better people.

You need to read. (You're off to a good start since you're reading this book...) You need to read widely with different topics and perspectives. You need to spend time going deep on issues of interest to you. Why? Because that's intellectual nutrition to help your mind develop well. Binging on online media is like eating only junk food all day long. You might be alive, but you're unhealthy and creating systemic problems that will cause you harm over time. It's the same with your brain; if you just fill it with superficial material, you'll develop long-term problems.

What's important for someone your age to recognize is that through reading, you can discover yourself more deeply. You can learn from others' experiences and ponder how you would have acted. You can tap into the accumulated wisdom of intelligent people for mere pennies. You can challenge yourself and find ways to improve. Wide exposure to the thoughts and experiences of others, distilled into books, helps accelerate your personal development.

Reading helps reduce stress, increases your knowledge, augments your vocabulary, improves your memory, hones your analytical and conversational skills, and sharpens your focus. By deeply learning about topics, you'll achieve a level of mastery and awareness that few possess. You'll be better off personally and professionally; people will enjoy your company and even pay you for your time. Successful people read a lot. You should, too.

TAKE THE LONG VIEW

MICHAEL PHELPS WAS USED to greatness; as an Olympian swimmer, he was routinely at the top of the stand to win the biggest medal. But for his final competition, he was denied his expected achievement in the 100-meter butterfly. Michael was bested by Joseph Schooling, a 21-year-old from Singapore.

It was a special, if a little awkward, moment for Joseph. You see, 8 years prior, as a 13-year-old boy, Joseph had asked Michael, whom he idolized, if he could take a photo with him during a training he attended in Singapore. Joseph aspired to be like this great swimmer and focused on the daily tasks that would lead him toward that goal. He was so intentional about his efforts that he surpassed his idol's abilities. That's dedication.

Having a focus on end results provides clarity and context for your daily decisions. Joseph wanted to be a great swimmer, so that influenced his behavior on an ongoing basis. He had small and simple things that he needed to do and repeat in order to pursue an end result he desired. Knowing what you want to become in life, personally and professionally, helps guide your thoughts and actions.

Taking the long view in life helps you tolerate failure and loss more easily. You're more likely to avoid destructive decisions that have long-term negative consequences because you understand that what you say and do today might have a ripple effect in the future. You become more tolerant, patient, and focused. You recognize that problems have a way of working themselves out, and you don't need to overreact or exhaust your emotional energy dealing with something that might be minor in the overall scheme of things.

A pilot flying toward a destination doesn't travel in a perfectly straight line. Gusts of wind and weather patterns might force small deviations along the way. But having a focus on the end result guides the pilot's actions, leading to minor course corrections to remain pointed in the right direction. Determine what destination you ultimately want in life and let that decision guide your thoughts and actions each day.

ADULTS ARE FAKING IT

MY FIRST JOB AS a teenager was working in a law office. I did basic secretarial grunt work for an attorney. It was very eye opening, and I was exposed to all kinds of very smart people. Or so I thought.

You see, being exposed to all kinds of professionals gave me the perception that these people "had it together." They had figured out life, and it was going well for them. They had unlocked the secrets of the universe sufficient to harness them in their favor. It was intimidating because here I was, an incompetent, immature, ignorant youngster. The chasm between where I was and where they were seemed enormous.

And that difference was daunting, giving me a bit of anxiety. How would I ever achieve what they had? How could I figure out how to "adult" like these competent people? Would I turn out to be a failure?

Fast forward to about a year ago. There I was, sitting in a room full of legal people, debating them on a policy that lets law enforcement steal property from people. (It's called civil asset forfeiture.) It was literally me against the rest of them:

police chiefs, sheriffs, prosecutors, and a smattering of other law enforcement representatives. I didn't have their credentials; I wasn't an attorney nor was I an expert at what they did.

But when I became an adult, I figured out what I didn't know as a teen. Adults are faking it. Even the ones with acronyms after their names or fancy diplomas or nice offices or hundreds of employees. There aren't any secrets of the universe to be unlocked. There's no playbook or life manual to be memorized. Adults are a hot mess, and they're still trying to figure out life. They've just gotten really good at projecting competence and effectively deceiving people into thinking they "have it together."

We often don't. And that should be motivating to you because the chasm isn't all that big. We adults have experienced more of life, to be sure, but so will you. And along the way, you'll come to realize that we're still incompetent, sometimes immature, and certainly ignorant. Be patient with yourself.

MANAGE YOUR EMOTIONAL REACTIONS

WE ADULTS HAVE AN advantage over you. Our brains are fully developed, and different areas of the brain trigger in response to a problem. Let's say, for example, that someone insults me in front of my friends. The *limbic* system in my brain, where emotions are processed, will likely urge me to scream and fight. But my *prefrontal cortex* is also activated, which plays a large role in decision making. It's the rational part of my brain, which helps keep unwise urges in check. In this instance, that portion of my brain will persuade me that it's not worth it to fight back, and that the better option is to ignore the other person and walk away.

Your disadvantage as a younger person is that your prefrontal cortex isn't fully developed, and it won't be until your mid-20s. Compounding the problem is that your brain is being bathed in hormones as your body matures, and these increased levels can influence you in ways you haven't yet experienced. This can lead to emotional outbursts and overreactions to problems that could have been handled more calmly.

Despite all of this, it's possible for you to manage your emotional reactions, since you aren't completely controlled by them. For starters, if you feel provoked or otherwise prone to an emotional outburst, pay attention to your breathing. Be conscious about making it slower and deeper. This alone will work wonders. Similarly, pay attention to your body; chances are, in these circumstances, your muscles are clenched and you're feeling stressed. So, as you breathe, intentionally relax your body from head to toes and think of each part as you focus on relaxing that part.

As you go through this exercise, it's important to pay attention to your feelings and process them, forcing your developing rational brain to pay attention to what's going on. Observe what you're feeling and why. Think of what provoked you and whether it's appropriate to respond, and, if so, how you should respond.

A final tip: exercise. Regular exercise works wonders for regulating your emotions and lifting you out of depressive feelings. Go for a run, clear your head, and process whatever problems are confronting you.

SEEK FIRST TO UNDERSTAND

WHEN WAS IN COLLEGE, I read Steven Covey's incredibly popular book *The 7 Habits of Highly Effective People*. One of the habits hit me upside the head: seek first to understand, then be understood. I was especially guilty of this explanation Dr. Covey gave: "Most people do not listen with the intent to understand; they listen with the intent to reply." In other words, we often tune out what the other person is saying or, rather, what they *think* and *feel*, until it's our turn to inject our opinion or state what *we* think or feel.

Teenagers are especially prone to act this way... at least, I was. (You probably are, too.) We think we "know it all," when, in reality, we know hardly anything. The primary benefit of seeking first to understand, then, is that it allows us to admit what's true: we don't understand very much. We're not in possession of all relevant information. By seeking to understand, by allowing others to teach us and help us learn from them, we become life-long learners and, thus, way more intelligent over time.

In addition to intelligence, you'll also increase in influence. The reason is simple but still can be surprising to see it in action. When you sincerely seek to understand the thoughts and feelings of others, you'll gain a rapport with them. They'll be more likely to confide in you. And when you speak, others will place more value in your words because they feel heard. They'll be more likely to take your suggestion, follow your direction, or fulfill your desires. You'll have shown that you care about understanding their point of view, so it becomes easier to take others on a journey from where they are (what they currently believe or do) to where you want them to be (what you want them to believe or do).

Fundamentally, all of this means not rushing to judgment. Don't make assumptions about others. Ask questions to gain understanding and give others the benefit of the doubt.

PAY IT FORWARD

THE RESTAURANT INDUSTRY WAS crippled by the government's response to COVID-19 in 2020. Many establishments were prohibited from opening their dining areas, forced to serve patrons only through the drive thru. Hoping to help in some small way, one man paid for his meal at a Dairy Queen in Brainerd, Minnesota, and then paid for the meal ordered by the person behind him.

This small act of generosity triggered a cascade effect, with over 900 people paying it forward over the course of 3 days, each one serving the one behind them. "During times like these, it kinda restores your faith in humanity a little," one customer said. "The way the world is now, you see a lot of anger, tension, and selfish behavior. What we witnessed was pure kindness, and it was a breath of fresh air really."

It may be hard to see at times, but your life is full of people serving you. Your parents go to great lengths to provide for and support you. People hold the door for you as you walk in the store. Strangers compliment you when they notice you dressing nicely or doing something well. Drivers yield so you can get where you're going. Friends pay for your meal. Life is full of these random acts of kindness.

It would be a shame if those demonstrations died after one cycle. Instead, they should inspire you to continue the cycle to benefit others. Seeing someone smile at you for no reason is reason enough to share our smile with others. Receiving homemade bread from a neighbor might lead you to bake some cookies for another neighbor.

In all things, remember that your life is heavily influenced by the sacrifice and service of others. Their generosity toward you should remind you of this debt, and, while you may not be able to literally repay those who support you, you can discharge this debt by "paying it forward" to help others along your way. Life is full of enough gloom, doom, and darkness, so share a little of the light you've been given to help others on their way.

CULTIVATE CURIOSITY

BY ANY STANDARD, ALBERT Einstein was a successful person. Considered the most influential physicist of the 20th Century, he's best known for developing the theory of relativity and winning the Nobel Prize for Physics. With a featherbed salesman for a father, and a stay-at-home mother, nothing in his upbringing necessarily suggested he would become who he did. But when he was 5 years old, he came across a compass and was fascinated by how the needle inside could be controlled by invisible forces. Through later study, he was able to focus on his interests and develop the knowledge that made him famous. But as he himself said, "I have no special talents. I am only passionately curious."

As Sir Ken Robinson said, "Curiosity is the engine of achievement." Successful people are curious. They wonder how things work and if they can be harnessed or improved. They challenge the status quo and think critically. People who are curious have a thirst for knowledge and ask basic questions: "What is this?" "How does this work?" "Why does this happen this way?"

Curiosity makes life better in three ways. First, you'll make better decisions in your life because you'll have more information about the way the world works. The more you understand the forces at play, the more you'll be able to leverage them in your favor. Second, curiosity helps you find new opportunities. Turning over rocks, looking behind closed doors, and searching in hidden places will reveal things that the average person cannot or will not access. And that leads to the final way curiosity makes your life better: by making it more interesting. You'll gain knowledge and insights on a wide range of issues, making your conversations more interesting and attracting all kinds of people to you. With new opportunities and better decisions along the way, your life will be more enjoyable and successful, merely by asking questions and seeking knowledge.

A word of warning: curiosity requires idle time for your mind to wander and imagine things. You need free time, and even occasional boredom, to facilitate curiosity. So, make sure you're not constantly entertained with an electronic gadget that prevents you from developing it.

SHOOT A GUN

BECOMING A SUCCESSFUL ADULT requires learning and practicing responsibility. It also requires personal discipline. Learning how to use a firearm is a great way at honing your skills in both these areas.

Guns are dangerous. So are matches, gasoline, vehicles, knives, and more. Any object that can cause harm to one's self or others should be treated with respect and handled carefully. In the right hands, these tools can be amazing and even life-saving. Indeed, countless people have been able to successfully defend themselves using a firearm against someone trying to harm them. Did you know the average response time for police after calling 911 is over 15 minutes? When you or a loved one is threatened, it would be helpful to have the means to thwart an attack.

But that won't happen if you don't have the means or knowledge to do so. Just as responsible adults own one or more fire extinguishers in their home in case of fire, the responsibility of self-defense means having the ability to stop an attack, should it occur.

Consider taking a class or having someone with ample experience teach you how to use a firearm. Spend time at a firing range using different firearms: handguns, shotguns, and rifles. Become familiar with the basic rules of safety, which will help you confidently handle dangerous weapons without posing a threat to yourself or anyone else. All guns should be treated as loaded. Never point the gun barrel at something you don't wish to destroy. Keep your finger off the trigger until you're ready to shoot. Be sure of your target and what's behind it.

When you learn to respect a powerful tool and treat it with care, you'll begin to internalize the importance of careful control, thoughtful action, and personal discipline. These values can be applied in other areas of your life to help you become a purposeful, responsible person.

KILL A CHICKEN

IT WAS COMMON PRACTICE for the indigenous people in North America to make use of every part of the buffalo they killed. The meat was used for food; the bones made into tools; skin turned into clothes and other items; hair used to stuff pillows or as rope; and much more. The people had a spiritual connection to the animals upon which they depended for their own lives. Suffice it to say, they knew exactly where their food came from.

Today, over 300 million Americans consume food produced by less than 1% of the population. This is an engineering feat and shows the power of the market. People are able to apply their labor to other pursuits and exchange it for food, rather than everyone having to farm and raise animals themselves. This is called a division of labor; some people are farmers, others mechanics, others authors, etc.

One of the downsides of this approach, however, is that people lose respect for the sacrifice that's made during the process. Loss of animal life was once treated with respect; now it's an industrial process where billions of animals are butchered in bulk. Meat is merely what's prepackaged in family-size portions at the store, a processed product that people don't even think about how it was prepared.

There's something to be said for being connected to the "circle of life," having a knowledge of and respect for the food chain that you're a part of. You'll gain a great amount of insight by participating in some fashion. Maybe that's touring a slaughterhouse in your area, or simply watching some YouTube videos about the process to see how it works and what's involved in providing the meat you consume.

But there's nothing like doing it yourself to give you some real-world knowledge. Chances are, you know someone who raises backyard chickens, or you might do it yourself. Ask to participate in the process of killing and processing one of the birds so you can better appreciate what happens and enjoy that delicious meal next time you're at Chick-fil-A.

DON'T BE AN AGEIST

A FRIEND OF MINE was recently sitting in a coffee shop and overheard a couple of women talking about ageism (prejudice against people based on their age) and the problems it creates for older people. For example, some older people struggle to find employment with companies who prefer younger candidates instead. But almost in the same breath, these women began talking about teenagers and how they were mostly "lazy," "entitled," and "aimless." I'm told it was a laughably hypocritical discussion.

I wonder what I would have said if I were sitting next to them! I wonder this because I was subjected to all kinds of ageism when I was younger. I've always looked younger than I am. I remember being pulled over as a 17-year-old driver by a police officer who thought a 13-year-old was joyriding in his mom's van. Job interviews were tough because I looked young, immature, and inexperienced. And as I transitioned into a new line of work, I found myself debating attorneys, elected officials, and other professionals who often discounted my views and knowledge because I was young.

But I knew my stuff in these meetings; I studied hard, learned the topics inside and out, and could hold my own in these discussions. Once, a government attorney dismissed my statements because I didn't have a law degree like her and was too young to have "gained enough experience." This was a logical fallacy, of course, and she was avoiding responding to my actual statement by pointing to my age.

Someone's views are not correct or worth more consideration just because they're older than me. On the other hand, wisdom comes through experience, which only comes with age. It's a fine line to walk, but one's age doesn't necessarily mean anything. What matters is the truth, regardless of the age of the person expressing it. Bad ideas and biases can come from people both young and old. Learn to recognize truth from all sources, even young people. Study hard and become a beacon of truth as well, even at a young age.

ABOLISH THE VICTIM MENTALITY

ONE HUNDRED AND FOUR people were divided into two groups as part of a study at Stanford University. One group was told to write a short essay about a time when they felt bored, and the other group wrote about a time in their life that seemed unfair. After writing their essays, each person was asked a few questions, including whether they would be willing to help with a simple task.

Participants who wrote about being wronged by someone were 26% less likely to help, and researchers observed that on average they were 13% more entitled and 11% more likely to express selfish attitudes. (They were also more likely to steal the researchers' pens!) While merely a study of human behavior, it shines a light of how destructive the victim mentality can be.

While there are actual victims in cases such as fraud or abuse, someone who adopts a victim mentality creates imagined circumstances in which their misfortune or suffering is a result of the perceived actions of others. This type of person believes they've been wronged without any fault of their own and that they're not responsible in any way for their circumstances. They act selfishly to encourage others to feel sorry for them and leverage the pity and reassuring compliments of others to compensate. This is emotionally draining for the person's family members, friends, and associates, and ultimately creates a cycle that's difficult for the person to break.

Embracing a victim mentality allows a person to gain attention and avoid responsibility. It also inhibits growth because, rather than seeing problems as temporary hurdles that can be overcome, a person begins to see them as insurmountable obstacles that others have deliberately placed in their path. Blame, finger-pointing, and pity parties are tools of the trade, and are surrounded by pessimism, fear, and anger.

You must abolish this mentality. Recognize that others aren't "out to get you," nor are they the reason for any misfortune you may experience. Life is full of obstacles, and your growth will come from learning how to, instead, embrace a survivor mentality, where you learn how to overcome obstacles and become increasingly confident, healthy, and successful.

SHOW UP EARLY, STAY LATE

HAVE YOU EVER BEEN around someone who's needy? Perhaps you have a friend or family member who's always asking you to help with or give them something. It can be draining after a while, always feeling like you're being "used" by another person.

Relationships are a lot like a bank account. You can't really make withdrawals until you've made deposits. If you want to take something out, you have to first put enough in. People who are constantly asking for something without giving something in return are like someone whose bank account is empty, always asking to borrow money because they're broke. This is a bad way to manage your finances, and it's a bad way to manage your relationships.

Instead, be proactive about "making deposits" in your interactions with others. Hold a door open for your mom or offer to carry something for your sibling. Offer help to a teacher or see if a friend needs a hand with something. One of the best ways to instill this mindset in yourself is to make it a point to show up early to any meeting you attend and stay late. Getting there ahead of time will show the event organizer (or teacher, church leader, or whomever) that you care and want to see the event succeed. You can help them reduce stress by offering to take care of any last-minute tasks. You'll be contributing rather than simply attending. Similarly, by staying late, you show that you're not just "transactional" in your relationship, only there to gain something for yourself. You can help take down chairs, take out the trash, or clean something up. You'll be making some significant deposits in that relationship. Even though they're simple, they're meaningful.

By developing this habit, you'll have strong relationships that will allow you to make "withdrawals" as needed. When you need help with something, others will be eager to come to your assistance. They'll want to give back to you, and that will benefit you over the long term.

DISTRACT YOURSELF TO DELAY GRATIFICATION

PARENTS OFTEN TALK TO their children about the dangers of instant gratification, immediately seeking a reward for good behavior, spending the money they just earned, etc. This can develop a destructive attitude that prevents them from saving their money for the future, working hard for a reward that will come later, or making a short-term sacrifice that may have a long-term benefit. Learning how to delay gratification is an important part of becoming a successful adult.

But temptations are everywhere, especially when they can order something online with a couple clicks and have it delivered the next day! So how do they delay gratification and reduce the desire to always get what they want when they want it? The answer may lie in a study where dozens of children were given two marshmallows, side by side. The researchers told each child that they would leave the room for a little while then return, and if they ate the first marshmallow before they got back, the child couldn't eat the second.

One group of kids was told to imagine, while the researcher was gone, how marshmallows are similar to puffy, white clouds. Another group was told to imagine how soft and sweet they were. Finally, a third group was encouraged to think of pretzels and how salty and crunchy they were. Interestingly, the children in the first group were able to wait almost three times longer before indulging in the first marshmallow than the children who were thinking about how delicious they would taste.

More interesting, however, is the group that thought of pretzels, which have nothing to do with marshmallows. These kids had the longest delay of gratification; thinking of something they couldn't have distracted them even more than trying to actively resist the temptation in front of them. In other words, we best delay our gratification by finding ways to distract us from the temptation in front of us. So, when you find yourself presented with something you should probably avoid, don't just employ willpower to resist it. Instead, send your attention elsewhere by imagining a different pleasure and focusing your mind on something else entirely.

NO ONE OWES YOU ANYTHING

YOU MAY HAVE HEARD stories before about how baby birds are sometimes pushed out of the nest to force them to learn to fly, leaving the comfort of their familiar home behind them. With songbirds in particular, the parents are often able to induce the younglings to leave a safer nest for a dangerous life before they might be ready. Consider the opposite scenario: mature birds still in their nest, expecting their mother or father to continue caring for them. It's absurd and unnatural.

You probably know some people in your social circles who cling to dependency, young adults who haven't "left the nest" and continue to expect their parents to support them. And, frankly, there are millions of adults who are still unnecessarily dependent and expect taxpayers, via the government, to provide for their needs. This type of entitlement mentality is infectious and enticing, but it will severely undermine your self-confidence and professional success.

The raw truth is that no one owes you anything. You're not owed good health, happiness, success, comfort, or freedom from pain and problems. No one owes you a house, a bed, or even a single meal. As an adult, you won't be entitled to anything in life. The reason is simple: an entitlement means that someone else has a duty. If you're "owed" free health care, then that means others have a duty to pay it (which they don't). If you feel entitled to free college, subsidized housing costs, or welfare support, then someone else has to pay for all these things for you (which they don't). You're responsible for yourself, so don't try to shift the responsibility to others.

Once you're at a point where you can start leaving the nest, either for temporary trips or permanently, you need to find your own food. Don't rely on mother bird to keep sustaining you. Actively look for opportunities to sustain yourself.

And by accepting the reality that life owes you nothing, you'll come to understand that everything you *do* have is a blessing. You'll see what you've been able to create or work hard to obtain, and you'll feel deeply satisfied. You'll be the confident captain of your own ship, rather than a stowaway on someone else's.

RECIPROCATE

IN A WELL-KNOWN RESEARCH study, participants were asked to take part in an experiment on "art appreciation" alongside another person. What they didn't know was that the other person was a research assistant, and that the study had nothing to do with art. At one point in the pretend art experiment, the assistant left the room during a brief break. In some cases, the assistant returned with a drink for himself and the study subject, saying "I asked [the researcher] if I could get myself a Coke, and he said it was okay, so I bought one for you, too." In the other cases, the assistant returned emptyhanded and the experiment continued.

As the experiment concluded and the art had been reviewed by the participants, the disguised assistant then asked the subject to do him a favor. He said he was selling raffle tickets and asked the subject to buy some, as he was hoping to win a prize for selling enough. Perhaps feeling like they owed him something, the subjects for whom a drink had been purchased were twice as likely to buy raffle tickets than the other subjects.

Plenty of other research makes clear that humans are likely to reciprocate for those who do something for them; we feel indebted to those who've done something for us. And you can use this fact for your own purposes, by doing things for (or giving things to) other people who you later want to help you with something.

But beware that you don't make this a transactional and deceitful situation, in which you're only helping in order to be helped. Be genuine and meaningful about your relationships, even though you understand that the rule of reciprocity will lead these people to help you as needed throughout your life. And recognize that you yourself will do things for others because they've once done something for you. This is how strong relationships of mutual exchange are built.

FAIL FORWARD

SOME OF THE MOST successful people first failed several times. J.K. Rowling is one of many famous failures, having been rejected by a dozen major publishing companies before finally finding someone to publish her first Harry Potter book. Steve Jobs was fired from the company he created, only to later return to save Apple and lead it into an amazingly successful future. Peter Thiel is widely regarded as a successful entrepreneur—he was the first outside investor in Facebook and later sold his shares for over a billion dollars—but the hedge fund he started, Clarium Capital, lost billions of dollars in assets.

Successful people have a mindset that sees failure as progress, not merely an obstacle, but an opportunity to learn. Just as resistance is what grows muscle, such as lifting weights at the gym, making mistakes creates a stronger person because it enriches your life experience and gives you more insight and wisdom.

Of course, this isn't to say that you should seek out failure. Quite the opposite, actually. You should remain focused on your goals and let them give you direction for your daily actions. But along the way, as you *mess* up, don't *give* up. Instead, remain focused on the goal and assess what went wrong and what needs to be fixed so you can still succeed.

This goal-oriented approach is also called failing forward. Many people, when faced with a problem, stop their momentum or even go in reverse. They shrink into themselves or turn around and go back to where they started. But failing forward means persevering, recovering from failure and applying what you've learned to keep going, keep trying, keep working toward your goal.

The secret about failure is that improvement follows or, at least, the opportunity for you to improve, if you're willing to apply what you've learned from failure. Experiences where things don't go your way can teach you how to improve the next time you come across a similar situation. You'll also learn about yourself through the importance of failure, about how much pain you can endure or how resourceful, strong, and intelligent you truly are.

UNPLUG

HOW OFTEN DO YOU use a phone, tablet, computer, or other device each day? Pause and think about it and try to do the math. If you're at all close to the average of teenagers in the United States, it's more than 7 hours each day, and that doesn't include time spent using screens for school and homework. That's pretty astounding, right?

Our devices are amazing productivity tools. We can be in close communication with friends and family no matter where we are, and the world's information is at our fingertips. But like any tool, these devices have their downsides, and we should be aware of them to ensure they're used properly.

Just as it's hard to "see the forest for the trees," in other words, understand the overall situation when you're in the middle of it, it can be difficult to see the impact technology and screen time is having on your life until you take a step back. And that's why periodically unplugging is important so you can find the right balance for your life. Taking the time to intentionally abstain from using your devices is a healthy, simple "reset" to focus on other aspects of your life.

How long can you last without your device? A few hours? A full day? Don't just let the device sit there taunting you. Actively focus your attention on a project or experience that will allow you to deeply focus and think. Go camping. Play some sports. Make a craft. Bake something. Whatever it is, give yourself prolonged opportunities to be away from your device to better live in the present, connect with those around you, and have time for your brain to process your own thoughts instead of constantly being bombarded with others' thoughts.

In a nutshell, refuse to let technology run your life. Show yourself that you can control this constant connection by turning it off from time to time. Doing so will improve your mental health, your relationships, and your ability to focus on what matters most to you.

IT'S OKAY TO ASK QUESTIONS

"THERE'S NO SUCH THING as a stupid question." You've heard this from a young age, from parents and teachers, yet too often people don't believe it. They think that needing help is a sign of weakness, that they don't deserve help, or they prefer to wait for someone else to ask instead. But these self-limiting beliefs are totally backwards.

Research shows that those who seek advice are likely to be thought of as *more* competent. In one study, participants were asked to communicate and do brain teasers with an unseen partner using a computer. At the end of the experiment, they were asked to rate their partners on different criteria, including how competent they thought the other person was. The unseen partners were scored higher for competency when they asked for help or advice. (As it turns out, these partners didn't exist; the participants were only interacting with a computer that was programmed to respond to participants in various ways.) In other words, asking for help may actually lead the other person to see you as more competent, perhaps since you have the emotional maturity to seek knowledge and the confidence to ask in order to acquire it.

Consider a couple examples. Instead of worrying that your coach might find out you can't perform a certain move and remove you from the team, show the coach how committed you are and how hard you practice by asking him for tips on how you can improve. Or if something is bothering you and you wish someone would ask you how you're feeling, instead, approach a close friend or family member and ask them directly if you can share something personal with them.

By contrast, think of a person who's so nervous or timid or embarrassed that they tend not to ask for help. They wander through life uncertain of what to do, where to go, or how to do things because they'd prefer to not ask and remain ignorant rather than to seek support from others as they move forward in life. This person sounds miserable and unproductive. Let it be a warning sign to you: ask for help when you need it, and you'll move along further and better in life.

DON'T BE A HYPOCRITE

IN THE TIDAL MUDFLATS of Japan, you can find the mudskipper, a rather unusual fish that can scoot across land and absorb oxygen through its skin. These brownish creatures blend in with their muddy environment and aren't much to look at. In contrast to their slithering, simple life at all other times, the male mudskipper's mating performance presents an entirely different experience, an energetic display in which these tiny creatures launch themselves over a foot in the air over and over again, hoping to attract a female.

Coming across this story, I couldn't help but think of people I knew growing up who would put on their own performance of sorts, hoping to attract attention from their crush. They would act quite differently, as if in character, presenting themselves in a way that they thought would be most pleasing to the other person. These are hypocrites, and the word's origin makes it even clearer. It comes from the Greek *hypokritēs*, which means a 'stage actor,' or someone acting as someone else.

You surely know people like this who want to be liked by others, so they say whatever they think will earn them attention and praise from those around them. Can you imagine how exhausting it is to live like this? To always be assessing the audience and modifying your behavior accordingly? These people may earn attention in the short term, but it's a game that can't be kept up over the long term. Hypocrites are eventually unmasked, and people see who the person really is. We love actors when we know it's a performance, but no one is a fan of fake relationships in real life.

Don't pretend to be something you're not. Eventually, the other person will get to know the "true you" and you'll be caught in your deception. Instead, be authentic, and you'll attract people who'll want to be with the real you, no performance required.

YOU'RE NOT GREAT THE WAY YOU ARE

WE NOW LIVE IN a world where mere existence is celebrated; out of a desire to be "inclusive," no one wants to offend anyone else. Thus, we have campaigns for "equity" that give to "disadvantaged" people things they haven't earned, because of some supposed unfairness that exists.

These efforts seem to affirm that it's okay for people to remain as they are—that their current state should be celebrated and supported. If they're not educated enough or don't work hard enough or can't create enough value—that's okay! They still deserve to make a "living wage" and are entitled to whatever they need, to be provided for everyone else.

This message creates a mindset that leaves young people woefully unprepared for the real world and the truth: not everyone is a winner. Simply showing up isn't enough. You have to apply yourself and work hard. It's up to you to excel.

It may feel good to be told that you're great the way you are, that you're good enough as is. And the people sharing this message may feel like they're simply trying to affirm that each person matters. Sure, that's true; everyone has worth. But that doesn't mean there isn't room for improvement. It doesn't mean you're good enough as is. Chances are, you're not.

At any age, but especially as teenagers, we're still in development, always progressing (which direction that's in is up to us). Think of yourself as a partially constructed project. You're a building that needs its foundation reinforced with more concrete and steel. Your windows need some washing, and your smelly bathroom needs a deep cleaning. The roof has a few leaks that need attention, and some rooms have gathered several layers of dust.

There's no better way to promote mediocrity than to tell someone they're good enough the way they are. You have a wealth of untapped potential that remains to be discovered and developed. Aim to be better tomorrow than you were today.

BE JUDGMENTAL

IT'S COMMON TO HEAR people criticize being judgmental, casting it in a negative light only. And it makes sense why the concept of judging others gets such a bad rap. It brings up memories of bullies sidelining you because of how you dress, being made fun of for wearing braces, or not being considered very popular because your family is poor or different in some noticeable way. Clearly, being judgmental can be a tool of bullies.

But tools aren't inherently bad. Firearms can both attack others wrongly or defend against an aggressor; matches can burn your home or be a critical means of keeping warm; and the Internet can be a source of great enlightenment or horrible exposure to awful things. Being judgmental is also a tool, one of discernment, that also has a positive side. And that's where we should be using it, and often.

As you grow up, it's important to be a good judge of character. You want to associate with people who will be a good influence on you. You should avoid toxic people who will drag you down or involve you in bad things. Being judgmental of others allows you to make more informed decisions that will improve your life.

Making judgments also gives you the opportunity to compare and contrast others' personalities and behaviors with your own. This helps you understand your weak and strong points, and where you can develop yourself to improve. You can harness your strengths and build on your weaknesses, by observing and judging how these traits look in others.

Being judgmental is basically about being selective in whom you associate with, how you spend your time, what you spend your money on, and all the other decisions you make. We constantly make judgments: what food we prefer; the clothing we want to wear; how seriously we want to take our studies; what music we listen to; whether we will develop a friendship with someone; and so much more.

These judgments are necessary in order to live a productive life with limited time and resources. What's important, though, is that we don't use the tool poorly, basically, that we're not a jerk about the judgments we make. Compassion can still exist while we make judgments that help inform our decisions.

YOLO

I RECENTLY CONNECTED WITH a friend who revealed during the conversation that she had never left the state she lived in. I couldn't comprehend this; there's a whole world out there to explore! (And the reason wasn't the family's finances; they had enough to travel if they wanted.) Years had gone by with normal schedules and predictable days, but, for her, they were apparently free from adventure, exploration, learning new skills, and developing hobbies. Her life sounded pretty boring.

We only have one life to live. (Or, as the kids these days say, YOLO.) That's why, for a long time, there's been a related saying: "There's no time like the present." If we procrastinate actually living life, then what are we living for?

Let's be clear about one thing: the YOLO mindset has been used by some to justify reckless behavior and being totally irresponsible. That's not being adventurous; it's simply being immature. Don't fall for the trap. Because we "only live once," we should be responsible and cautious in what we do, since we want our one life to be a long one. But within those boundaries, we can pursue all kinds of interesting activities and adventures.

And while you're young, you're able to take on way more risk because you're not burdened with business obligations, a mortgage, children, and bills. You can travel, start up a new business, obsessively pursue a new hobby, or whatever catches your interest. And looking back on your life a decade or two (or five) from now, what will you be happy you did? What will you regret not having done?

Don't delay for another day (or decade) what you can dive into now. Take risks, go on adventures, plan new things, and expand your horizons. Do it safely, but do it.

SPEAK THE TRUTH, NOT YOUR TRUTH

IT'S BECOME FASHIONABLE IN recent years for young people to refer to "their truth" when discussing an issue. "I've been trying to live my truth lately," one might say. Or when disagreeing, another might say "Your truth is your truth, and my truth is mine." With praise, one might tell a friend "I admire the way you speak your truth."

This is nonsense. In reality, what these ignorant individuals are really referring to is a combination of their opinion and experience, but these things don't spontaneously create truth. Plenty of people can believe and desire things that aren't true. Just because you think something is (or should be) a certain way does not make it "your truth."

Saying it this way is intentional, though. By saying something is "their truth," a person is implicitly trying to make it so that you cannot argue with them. Who are you to question "their" truth? It's *theirs*, not yours. This approach treats truth as subjective, meaning that it depends on each person's experience, understanding, or feelings.

But that's not how truth works. It's not subjective; it's objective, which means that it exists and is observable by others. It's true that heavy objects fall to the ground, that power tends to corrupt, and that inflation robs people of their hard-earned money. These things aren't subject to people's opinions and feelings; they're objectively true.

Imagine that a crime happens, and that you're called into court as a witness. Raising your right hand, you're then asked if you swear to tell "your truth"? That's ludicrous. Either the crime happened, or it didn't. Either you saw the person do something wrong, or you didn't. This reality shouldn't depend on what your feelings or opinions are.

Reject the idea that each person has their own truth because a society built on a subjective treatment of truth is one that will quickly crumble. You can't trust or work well with people if they reject reality in favor of their own delusional fantasies.

READ KARL MARX. THEN THROW IT IN THE TRASH.

COMMUNISM IS RESPONSIBLE FOR killing more than a hundred million people in the last century, and the Titan of Terror responsible for planting the seeds of tyranny is Karl Marx, whose *Communist Manifesto* launched a train wreck of carnage across the world. This 1848 book contains revolutionary ideas that were widely popular at the time, resonating with a working people who looked jealously at the property and wealth of others, and embrace a political system they were falsely told would bring equality and justice.

As the saying goes, those who don't learn from the past are condemned to repeat it. That's why it's important to expose yourself to awful ideas that have influenced countless people to commit atrocities. Reading the writings of Karl Marx and other socialist revolutionaries helps us understand the emotional appeals they relied on, the perspective they had, and the way they successfully persuaded millions to support their proposed system of government.

Today, many of your peers are embracing these ideas. One national survey found that 70% of young people are likely to vote socialist, and that 1 in 3 have a favorable view of communism. That's staggering, and it likely stems from ignorance about history. Of course, it's tempting to support ideas that claim to give you free things: education, health care, housing, food, and more. Who doesn't want the easy life?

The problem is that these ideas are false promises, and studying history is the way we learn this reality. By reading the writings of Marx and his peers, we see how the same temptations seduced people in past generations, and then by learning the outcome of socialist and communist political systems, we can see how these seductions led to widespread destruction and death.

So, read up on Marx and his ideological allies. Understand what envy looks like when turned into a political system. Learn the false promises of socialism and the destruction that they inevitably bring. Then throw this morally bankrupt drivel into the trash and get to work fighting for a world that rejects such bad ideas.

LIFE ISN'T BLACK AND WHITE

WHEN I WAS YOUNGER, I had a pretty well-defined list of likes and dislikes. I knew what was what, and that was that. I loved root beer and hated drinking plain water. I loved watching cartoons but hated animé. I loved spending money but hated having to earn it. Things were pretty binary: options between black and white, opposites that didn't change and were well defined.

That spilled over into other areas of life, where my binary thinking led me to conclude that certain people were good, and others were evil; some ideas were right, and others were flat-out wrong. There were two sides, and I had to determine which was which. This way of thinking led me to not see things very clearly. Let's use an example to illustrate.

Back in the days of using film, you could develop your own photos. I did this for a photography class and had a small room where I could block out the light and use equipment to shine some light through my film onto the paper below. That paper went into a liquid solution which would allow the paper to react to the light. The stronger the light, the darker the reaction, thus, creating all shades of black to create the ultimate picture.

I messed up several times in this process. Sometimes, I exposed way too much light, causing the photo to be all black. In other situations, nothing showed up on the white paper. These ruined results didn't show me the interesting pictures I intended them to be. There was no variation, just total black or total white. It didn't make for good photography.

Thinking that life is black and white doesn't make for good thinking. Life is full of gray. Good people can do really bad things, and seemingly evil people can have some redeeming qualities. Bad decisions might have good aspects, and good intentions might lead to bad outcomes. Yes, you need to be careful about the "gray areas" of life, so you don't end up making bad choices leading to a blackened conscience. But people are complicated, and so are their choices; let's tolerate and appreciate the variations in life and recognize that binary thinking won't help us see things clearly.

DEVELOP A PRACTICAL SKILL

"THE WORLD IS FULL of very happy septic-tank cleaners and miserable investment bankers."

Those are the words of Mike Rowe, whose hit TV show *Dirty Jobs* chronicled his attempts to engage in all kinds of weird, dangerous, and, yes, dirty jobs. It makes for fun watching, but for Mike, it's turned into a mission: helping young people pursue meaningful work using their hands.

Many of the best opportunities require a skill, not a piece of paper from a costly university. You can make some really good money as a carpenter, plumber, welder, or in any number of other trades. And even if you don't make a job out of it, skills like these will save you money building or repairing your own property, and you'll be of service to others who might need your skilled help in the future.

And being able to create something with your own brains and hands is a remarkable feeling that will empower you and increase your self-confidence. Learn how to make a website, create a chicken coop, design a landscape, build a shed, become a chef, or something else. Having the know-how to do something that's useful and help-ful will be a rewarding feeling, and if you're inter-ested, you can monetize that skill by working in that field full time, having a side hustle for extra income, or starting your own business to have in-creased independence in life.

Most kids sit in class and do what they're told. They're on a conveyor belt having all kinds of stuff crammed in their heads that they don't care about and will never use. They find a minimum wage job doing something that doesn't require much skill, if any, and they fritter away their life. Don't do that. Jump off the conveyor belt. Be intentional about your life. Choose specific skills you find enjoyable, rewarding, and potentially lucrative. Focus on what you want to learn, find someone to help, identify the resources you need, then be per-sistent in working toward your goal. Be relentless about improving and increasing your knowledge and experience.

CREATE VALUE FOR OTHERS

IMAGINE THERE'S A COMPANY you'd love to work for. Let's say, for example, that it's a snowboarding apparel company, and snowboarding is your favorite hobby. You'd love to be on their marketing team to connect with social influencers and other companies to promote their products and snowboarding in general.

Now think of how most people pursue a job like that: they write a poorly designed resume, send in an application following the company's standard process, wait to hear back, and hope for the best. Instead, what if you followed the company's leadership team on social media, sent a gift to the CEO (perhaps something new/innovative in the industry you think they would enjoy), emailed the marketing director an e-book you created to showcase what you could do for the company, tagged them in a social media post talking about what a great job they're doing, and started a blog where you positively reviewed their products or services?

It's obviously no question which person would come to the attention of that company's leadership. Of all suggestions to share about how to succeed in life, this one ranks near the top: create value for others. Think of how other people could be benefitted by your efforts. Serve, share, and think outside the box about how to go the extra mile. It's effectively the Golden Rule: treat others as you would want to be treated if you were in that position. If you were needing to hire stellar people, wouldn't you want to find people who think outside the box and put in an effort to show how serious they are about wanting the job?

Whether it's for work or your personal life, creating value for others will generate positive sentiment toward you as a person, and will also induce the other person to feel a desire to reciprocate, thereby bringing you success as well. At the end of the day, all relationships are built upon mutual interest, and the more you show you're interested in others by creating value for them, the more they'll want to serve and support you.

DON'T KEEP UP WITH THE JONESES

YOU'VE PROBABLY HEARD THE phrase, "The grass is greener on the other side of the fence," a reference to how people often think that circumstances other than their own would be better, or that they're missing something that could be better. We look at others' social media profiles and see popularity, happiness, and friendship, while we're stuck at home sulking, feeling lonely. We see someone with financial success flouting their wealth, while we're barely scraping by. It happens as teens, and it continues as adults.

It actually gets worse as you age. As you earn more money and can incur debt, this "grass is greener" mentality takes on a sinister twist where people often feel the need to follow in the footsteps of others to be more like them or obtain the same status. If your neighbor gets a boat, then, suddenly, you need one, too. That fancy car your friend got? Now you're thinking of getting your own. Fancy frequent vacations? That's something you need to do, not just your co-worker. Right?

Yeah, some people are simply happier or wealthier than you. There always will be. But people often project these things with a false front. They're often not truly happy; they're just posing with a picture-perfect smile for the Instagram photo. Or they're not actually wealthy; they're deep in debt and can't afford the new toy they bought. Yet these superficial and visible examples pressure others into pursuing the same things in hopes of obtaining the same apparent enjoyment or success that's being shown so publicly.

Resist the urge to act like others. Think thoughtfully about what *you* want and why. Don't change your behavior based on what you see others doing because they may be motivated by bad reasons. Live within your means and save as much as possible. Avoid debt.

And most importantly, don't think that others are happy and successful just by what you see on the surface. Chances are that their "green grass" is spray-painted just to make others *think* it's green.

DON'T CAUSE A CAR ACCIDENT

OVER SEVEN MILLION CAR accidents happen each year on U.S. roads alone, and nearly 40% of them are because of rear-end collisions. And of those, 87% happened because the driver wasn't paying attention to the road in front of them. Sadly, what that means is that millions of accidents were preventable, including the thousands of deaths and hundreds of thousands of injuries that results.

These accidents are often caused by texting while driving, speeding, or simply "tailgating," following the car in front of you too closely. And what these accidents ultimately mean is that the person causing them wasn't being responsible and thinking of others' safety.

The lesson here isn't just about cars, of course. Our behavior inherently affects other people. What we do can cause harm (or even death!) to others if we're not careful. Accidents are a part of life; we'll never be rid of them, and they're completely understandable when they weren't preventable with basic good behavior.

But when an accident is caused because of irresponsible behavior? That's a big problem. And you don't want to be in that situation when you're in control of a fast-moving machine or using the tiny one in the palm of your hand. Think of how awful you would feel if you injured or killed another person. You'd be sick with self-loathing and regretful about your actions. You wouldn't be able to find the words to comfort the victim or the victim's family. You would wish for the ability to rewind time and do better.

The point here is to be considerate of others. Act in a way that won't cause problems for others. Be thoughtful about those around you and what they might be going through. Spare your future self all the grief that comes from irresponsible behavior and decide to behave in a way that will help you and others be safe and successful in life.

LIFE IS A JOURNEY WITHOUT A DESTINATION

"MOM, ARE WE THERE yet?!"

It's a sentence that has slipped from our lips too many times to tell, whether we were running errands or on vacation. We're often impatient to get to where we're going and focused on the destination. Life, it seems, becomes a series of destinations; we're always planning to go somewhere or do something next.

But there's danger in always looking ahead. Think of when you're at a party, dance, or other social event, and you're talking to someone you're really interested in getting to know better. But during the conversation, they keep looking over your shoulder, darting their eyes around the room, in case they spot someone else they'd rather be talking with. How does that make you feel?

Contrast that against a conversation where it's clear the other person is focused on you. They're genuinely interested in what you're saying; they're asking you questions to learn more, and their body language conveys a concentration that makes you feel valued. How does *that* make you feel?

A person with this level of emotional intelligence knows that there are probably more interesting people to be talking with and other destinations they'd rather explore. But that doesn't mean that their current situation isn't worth soaking in and enjoying. They know, perhaps, that life becomes tiresome and unfulfilling if it's merely a series of future goals, rather than opportunities to enjoy what's in front of them now.

You might call this the "stop and smell the roses" lesson, a reminder to not take for granted the things we have in our life right now. There will always be new opportunities, decisions to make, and changes to implement... but the moments you have today are fleeting and will soon be forgotten. Take the time to make the most of these moments. Write in your journal. Take a photo or shoot a quick video to remember. Spend time in deep conversation with a friend or family member. Make memories with someone, or simply yourself, that will be treasured in the future. Life is a journey, and looking back on your life, you'll want to have enjoyed each step along the way.

AVOID ADDICTIONS

I ONCE NEEDED TO attend a very early morning meeting with a colleague of mine. But before we got on the road, this person requested that we stop at the local gas station. I obliged, and this person soon emerged from the shop with a very large container of soda, a sugary, caffeinated hit at 7am. They sheepishly explained that they couldn't start their day without this drink. They were addicted.

This isn't a crazy story, since millions of people are in the same situation, albeit with a caffeinated beverage that's hot instead of cold. Countless people line up at Starbucks and other stores each morning to start their day with this drug-induced assistance. And if you know anyone who's tried to kick their caffeine addiction, they'll share stories about how awful it was with shaking, anxiety, headaches, irritability, and more.

Caffeine is, of course, a socially acceptable drug. There are many more drugs to which people become addicted. Tons of people are addicted to pornography. Many more are addicted to their electronic devices. We consume things that trigger chemical reactions in our brains that are pleasurable. But these reactions become dependencies over time and end up controlling us.

And that's why addictions are to be avoided. It's far better to act than be acted upon. A person in control of their life can make clear decisions and act as they please. Someone who is controlled by something else often wastes significant time and money, avoids certain relationships, misses opportunities, and more. They don't succeed to the degree that they might were they free from the chains of their addiction, whatever it may be.

Some addictions are absolutely worse than others, but even seemingly harmless ones, such as video games, can be huge time wasters that prevent you from focusing on gaining an education, developing skills, and creating relationships that will lead you to be significantly successful as you mature. Avoid addictions like the plague so that you remain in control of your life, free to choose whatever's best for you.

SERVE INSTEAD OF SULK

IF YOU ASK TEENAGERS, they'll tell you they have it pretty rough. Research indicates that more teens are claiming boredom than ever before, despite an abundance of opportunity and easy and immediate access to the entire body of knowledge in the world, accessible at their fingertips. Thirteen percent of U.S. teens (over 3 million of them) said they had experienced at least one major depressive episode in the past year, up from 8% just a few years before. Anxiety and self-confidence issues cripple countless youth, and each problem (relationship drama, academic performance, financial struggles, and more) seems significant.

When you're faced with challenges, don't give up; get busy! Maybe that means directly tackling the problem with a series of steps that you come up with, perhaps with the help of a family member or friend. This way, you can overcome your challenge and turn a weakness into a strength. Then, in the future, you'll be better able to deal with the same or a similar challenge.

But many problems we face can't be resolved so easily. Sometimes, we just have to let a problem exist and deal with it. Not everything can be solved with an action plan. So, what to do in those situations? Does it make sense to sulk and let the problem fester in our mind? Should we lament our problem and turn ourselves into a victim, becoming a negative person and affecting those around us?

The answer is obvious. But how, then, should we deal with problems that can't be quickly solved? Serve others. Tons of research backs up this simple truth that we all implicitly understand: when we help others, we feel better about ourselves. Our problems become far less significant when we help others deal with theirs. By turning our attention toward helping others, we trigger a "virtuous cycle" where a stronger relationship (created by helping others) leads to feeling better, which leads to an even stronger relationship, and so on. Life gets better by helping others.

Helping others not only feels good but it also *does* us good. Depression is lowered, happiness is increased, and our emotions are regulated to the point where our problems are much more easily dealt with. So, next time you feel like sulking, get out and serve others.

TRAVEL

THERE ARE PEOPLE IN the world who want you to be afraid. I wrote a book about this, titled *Feardom*, which highlights why the government and media want you to be scared. In a nutshell, people who are scared are more easily controlled. We can be manipulated by those who want power over us if we're worried and they have a supposed solution to our perceived problems.

Among the many things to fear, "the other" stands near the top, people who aren't like us. Those who live on the other side of the world, worship a different God, and have an unfamiliar culture are more easily seen as an enemy, especially when the media and politicians tell us these people are the problem. But what if this narrative were totally wrong?

The flip side of fear is understanding; by learning what we have in common with others, which is a lot, we quickly come to realize that despite any disagreements, they're likely not the enemy. (If anything, the enemy is those trying to manipulate us for their own gain.) And we soon see that the bubble we grew up in prevented us from understanding the bigger picture.

So, one antidote to this ignorance and the fears that it can produce is travel. Get out and see the world. Meet people from different cultures. Learn about their backgrounds and interests. Share meals with them, exchange photos, and make memories together. Find a "pen pal" or two. By exploring the world, you quickly begin to see how your life is a tiny thread in a very large tapestry, and by stepping back and looking at the other threads, you see the bigger picture for what it actually is.

There's something powerful about discovering this interconnectedness with others, our shared humanity, that helps us understand that we have so much in common, notwithstanding our differences. We all grow up in our own bubbles, limited in our worldview by the community we're in and the media we consume. Consciously decide to break free from the bubble to gain a more proper perspective on life. Travel is the ticket.

SOME THINGS DON'T LAST

I'M A PRODUCT OF public school. (My mom apologizes to this day for not homeschooling me, but it just "wasn't a thing" in California in the 1990s.) When I was graduating high school, I was convinced that I needed a class ring and letterman's jacket to memorialize and remember my experience. It was money well spent, in my mind, because that was the world I was part of and thought would always be important to me.

It soon wasn't. That "money well spent" was wasted. I soon discarded these items once in college, realizing how irrelevant they were to my life. They were symbols of the past that no one in my new life cared about. They gathered dust, just like my yearbook full of signed statements from friends and acquaintances I soon lost track of.

The lesson I learned was that many things don't last, including the importance I once perceived about those things. People I thought I would always be friends with faded out of my life (and I out of theirs) as new ones came into the picture. The world I never wanted to change because the status quo was familiar and comfortable always did, and I learned that that was okay.

It's hard to predict the future. We can't assume that the status quo will stick around. The only constant in life is that things will change. And because life moves on, you shouldn't cling to the way things used to be. Instead, you need to embrace change. Be willing to let go of things in your life; we all outgrow clothes as much as we do toys, hobbies, friends, and more.

You are the constant in your life, as other things and people come and go; so, focus on developing yourself. Sure, spend time with and create amazing memories with friends, but since they, one day, may no longer be part of your life, make sure to also discover and develop your own interests, personality, and character along the way. Think about your future self and make plans today for who you want to be and how you'll make it happen.

BE A FREE-RANGE KID

WHEN I WAS GROWING up, it was quite common for kids to roam the streets and have fun without being tethered to their parents. "Be home before sundown," was the basic directive given to younger children, with more freedom given to teens. But today, helicopter parenting has become pervasive, where adults hover over their offspring, demanding to know where they are and what they're doing at all times. Technology even facilitates this, allowing parents to track their kids and monitor their behavior closely.

On the other end of the spectrum, we have so-called "free-range parenting," which is silly because this used to be known simply as... parenting. But this approach favors giving young people a reasonable amount of independence so they can "spread their wings" and learn to fly, rather than being overly sheltered in the family nest.

The coddling of young people, helicopter style, has produced a generation of incompetent adults who have created the term "adulting" to describe the things they often are inexperienced at doing, having not flexed those muscles from a younger age. This silly resistance to embrace personal responsibility should be avoided at all costs.

Don't joke about "adulting"; instead, learn how to become a competent and productive adult. Learn how to operate basic home appliances. Create a calendar and manage your time. Track your spending and set a budget. Prepare your own food (and make some meals for your family!) and develop good eating habits. Exercise. Wash your own clothes. Travel somewhere with friends. Take control of your own education. Seek out opportunities to speak in front of groups and interact with adults.

These things can all start now. Be as free range as your parents permit. Embrace your partial independence and explore the world. Find things that make you uncomfortable to get outside your comfort zone. Being "free range" implies unpredictability; you don't have the surety of four walls enclosing you, but there's a whole world to be explored. And having the freedom and confidence to take advantage of that freedom will make you stronger, wiser, and more fulfilled.

DRESS THE PART

A FEW YEARS AGO, a younger friend of mine went through a bit of a slump in his life, you might say. He was stuck in a rut and looking to get out. He came across an article about the power of dressing up and decided to give it a shot, only as an experiment on a trial basis. He said the results were immediate and very noticeable. People smiled at him, which prompted him to smile more. He was more aware of his self-image, including his posture and even his body language, which led to improvements. And strangers (visiting tourists) would stop him to ask for directions. (He lives in a busy city.)

How you present yourself to the world is a method of self-expression, so what are you trying to say? Are you a lazy slob who has low confidence and apathy about life? Or are you an ambitious young person with confidence and curiosity about life? Are you projecting a disinterest in others, signaling that they should avoid you? Or are you inviting interaction from others to build connections and find how you can help one another level up in life?

The way you dress sends an impression; books, including this one, are often judged by their cover. So, it's vital that you recognize the importance of casting a good impression on those you want to help you along in life, be it a teacher, employer, colleague, or friend. And yes, dressing the part includes basic grooming standards, which many teens often awkwardly struggle with. Trim and clean your nails. Shower regularly and use deodorant generously. You know... the basics.

But as my friend saw, dressing well is just one aspect of what will improve your mood and help you become more confident. Offer a firm handshake. Develop good posture. Learn about the importance of body language. Smile and be pleasant toward others, since you never know what opportunities you'll be presented with in life by those you interact with; so, don't alienate those who can possibly help you achieve greatness.

TAXATION IS THEFT

IF YOU KNOW ME, you know that I can't not write a chapter like this. As Benjamin Franklin once said, "In this world nothing can be said to be certain, except death and taxes." This reality soon sets in for many teenagers who, when receiving their first paycheck, are stunned by how much of their hard-earned money was taken by the government. Welcome to life as an adult, folks.

As you get older, you'll come to observe the sad reality about society: many people are leeches. They want to drain your resources and think that their mere vote is enough of a moral basis to justify taking your money to pay for projects they support. They'll argue that such a process is "the price we pay for a civilized society," in an attempt to justify letting the majority of people vote to take whatever they want through taxes, without any limits on that power.

And if you try to explain that taxation is actually theft, that it's basically an extortion fee you pay to avoid being locked in prison, you'll be criticized as an ingrate who wants children to starve and old people to die. This taxpayer-funded socialism,

to which most of society is addicted, was sound-
ly criticized by the French economist Frédéric
Bastiat:

> Socialism, like the ancient ideas from which it
> springs, confuses the distinction between gov-
> ernment and society. As a result of this, every
> time we object to a thing being done by gov-
> ernment, the socialists conclude that we object
> to its being done at all. We disapprove of state
> education. Then the socialists say that we are
> opposed to any education. We object to a state
> religion. Then the socialists say that we want
> no religion at all. We object to a state-enforced
> equality. Then they say that we are against
> equality. And so on, and so on. It is as if the so-
> cialists were to accuse us of not wanting per-
> sons to eat because we do not want the state to
> raise grain.

Understanding what taxation really is and why
it's a problem helps us understand the role of government and the need to learn about our individual rights so we can protect them. Check out my
book *Lessons from a Lemonade Stand* for more on
this.

LEARN FROM THE PAST

LAST YEAR I PURCHASED a bunch of "social studies" history books used in public schools across the country in an effort to see what was being taught to young people about the American Revolution and the creation of the Constitution. I was appalled, but not surprised, with what I found.

Each of these books taught the superficial details of everything that happened. They explained who said what and when, key battles that occurred, and the basic details of the circumstances that unfolded. But there wasn't much substance; the most they typically said about the *ideas* involved were that the colonists were upset about being taxed without having representation in Parliament.

This is crazy! There was so much more to what happened. These books did a disservice to students who were required to learn from these books, because they learned nothing about things like: the Judeo-Christian influence on the Founding Fathers; the impact of the Enlightenment Era; the philosophy of classical liberalism and the political views expressed by John Locke and his contemporaries; the applied learning from the Greek and

Roman societies; and so much more. These are the ideas and concepts that have modern relevance and would help readers gain insight from the past.

You've no doubt heard the quote "Those who don't learn from the past are condemned to repeat it." So many of today's problems are echoes and repeats of similar dynamics in the past. But most kids today never learn from the past; they only learn *about* the past. And I believe this is intentional because if powerful people can keep the populace ignorance of the failed mistakes of yesterday, they can continue convincing them to repeat those mistakes today. (Leading to such nonsense as "Democratic socialism is different from all those failed attempts at socialism before!")

Don't be content with a superficial understanding of history (including your family's history!). Go deep and seek after wisdom that has relevance to our world today. Try to find patterns between what happened in the past and what's happening today. Learn from, not just about, the past so you can help our society avoid repeating mistakes.

YOU'RE LIKELY A CRIMINAL

RESEARCH SUGGESTS THAT THE average American is unwittingly guilty of violating major criminal laws every day. (See *Three Felonies a Day* by Harvey Silverglate for examples.) There are so many laws, many of them written very vaguely, which empowers bureaucrats to punish innocent people at their discretion, that even upstanding citizens can find themselves the target of their own government.

In *Atlas Shrugged*, Ayn Rand describes a dystopian future in which this is the reality where so many things are made a crime that the average person becomes a lawbreaking criminal. One of the characters asks:

> Did you really think we want those laws observed? We want them to be broken. You'd better get it straight that it's not a bunch of boy scouts you're up against... We're after power and we mean it... There's no way to rule innocent men. The only power any government has is the power to crack down on criminals. Well, when there aren't enough criminals one makes them.

One declares so many things to be a crime that it becomes impossible for men to live without breaking laws. Who wants a nation of law-abiding citizens? What's there in that for anyone? But just pass the kind of laws that can neither be observed nor enforced or objectively interpreted – and you create a nation of law-breakers – and then you cash in on guilt. Now that's the system, Mr. Reardon, that's the game, and once you understand it, you'll be much easier to deal with.

In a legal environment where victimless behavior is criminalized, the government becomes disconnected from any moral foundation; politicians punish people who have done no wrong. And it leads to people walking on eggshells, gently tiptoeing around life so as not to offend or upset those in power, hoping to avoid their ire.

Look, you're probably a criminal. So am I. But in a world like this, the only option we have is the authentic one. Act morally and ethically. Stand up straight and choose the right, with unimpeachable behavior that's clearly good to anyone with a brain. Sure, some people will still complain and even try to criminalize your actions, but you cannot control those individuals. Own yourself and act accordingly.

SPECIALIZE IN SOMETHING

LAST YEAR, OUR FAMILY was able to get a pool built in our backyard. The process took months and involved dozens of contractors, each with different specialties—from excavation and assembly to pouring concrete and balancing chemicals. It was fun for my kids to watch everything come together, and it was especially enjoyable for me since I didn't have to do any of that particular work.

This impression was on my mind because I had recently watched a video where a man built a pool all by himself. It took him a very, very long time, and the result was comparatively inferior to what I now had in my backyard. This guy's pool was small, poorer quality, and lacked many of the features and technology that mine had.

I'm not very handy. I have a lot of different skills, but when an appliance breaks (or when I need a pool built!), I call on someone else. I focus on where I have special knowledge and earn money that allows me to pay for others' help when I need it. This is called specialization or the division of labor.

Life is far more productive and enjoyable because we benefit from the specialized knowledge of other people. Car manufacturers are great at what they do, and thank goodness, so I don't have to ride my bicycle everywhere. Farmers have really dialed in how to grow their crops well, and I'm glad for that, because my backyard garden is laughable by comparison. Because people focus on their specialties, they can then invest in improving and innovating their products. This in turn serves other people who then exchange with them for what they need.

Lean into this. Don't worry about learning about everything. Instead, focus on one or a few talents or interests you have that can be useful to others. Find your niche audience who needs what you have to offer, learn how to market to them, and develop an expertise that will financially reward you so you can pay for other people to help you do the things you aren't as good at.

HACK YOUR EDUCATION

SCHOOLING ≠ EDUCATION.

This truism goes over the heads of many people who have been conditioned to believe that we learn at school, and that's just the way life is. But many people don't learn much at school. And even those who go to school learn a ton outside of its four walls. The highly regimented school structure can be helpful to some, but it also deprives many young people of the flexibility and freedom that would allow them to focus on what matters most to them and their future self.

Want to know how adults learn? We don't sit around reading textbooks all day. We don't have assigned projects arbitrarily stipulating what we must know and in what manner. We don't regurgitate memorized data for an exam, only to later forget it. No, adults learn by identifying a need or desire and then cobbling together disparate resources that will help them gain the knowledge they need to progress forward.

Here's what I mean. When my lawnmower wasn't working right, I had a need. If the problem were significant, I would have likely called an expert for help, but in this case, I thought I could handle it. I downloaded the owner's manual and watched several YouTube videos. This gave me the knowledge I needed to solve the problem. When I was curious why some entrepreneurs were so successful, I listened to podcasts, read a few books, took a few entrepreneur friends out to lunch to pick their brain, and attended an event put on for entrepreneurs so I could learn more about their mindset and behavior.

Hackers don't follow instructions set by others; someone's preprogrammed rules aren't always the best for you and your situation. Hackers focus on their goal and then gather the information and resources necessary to achieve it. And that's what you should do with your education, since it's what competent adults do. Identify what your needs and desires are, and then find the information and experiences that will help you achieve them. Whether you're young or old, this is the simple process that will help you be productive and prosperous.

BE SMART ABOUT DEBT

IF YOU'RE INVESTING YOUR money, then interest is great; you're putting your money to work for you. But if you're the one borrowing money, then interest is working against you every minute of the day and night.

Check this out: young Americans aged 18 to 23 have an average debt of $16,043. The next age bracket, age 24 to 39, rockets up to $87,448. Much of this debt is due to school loans (another reason to read my book *Skip College*, hint hint). But the average young adult also has thousands of dollars in credit card debt, too. Soon comes a mortgage, saddling you with three decades of additional debt, for which you'll pay hundreds of thousands of dollars just in interest to the bank. Cha-ching!

Debt isn't inherently problematic. If you can leverage it, debt can work in your favor. For example, if your profession really requires you to obtain a college degree, and if that profession will pay you a high salary, then it's likely worth the commitment to achieve the longer-term goal. (And you can then more easily pay it off early, if possible.) But many people go into debt without having a plan to pay it back promptly. Their bills balloon into huge payments that they owe to the bank, and if they fail to repay, they can slide into bankruptcy, ruin their credit, and sabotage their family's financial future.

There's what's known as "good debt" and "bad debt." Good debt is typically a low-interest loan that will help you build wealth, such as getting a mortgage (assuming the value of your home rises faster than the interest rate) or obtaining an education (that will help you gain skills that increase your income). Bad debt has a high interest rate, as with credit cards, and is typically used on goods or services that don't help you build wealth (such as going on vacation and billing it to your credit card or buying a new video game console).

When wisely used, debt can help you level up in life. Be smart about it and consider the total cost and future impact of the financial decisions you make.

PERSISTENCE PAYS PRETTY GOOD

THOMAS EDISON WAS A prolific inventor often remembered for his innovations with the light bulb. "I have not failed," he allegedly said later in life. "I've just found 10,000 ways that won't work." It's easy to look at a quote like that and think he's embellishing, but, in his case, he was being sincere. He struggled to identify the right material for the filament (the thin strip of metal that's heated to produce light). "Before I got through, I tested no fewer than 6,000 vegetable growths, and ransacked the world for the most suitable filament material," he said. And over the course of 2 years, he tested "at least three thousand theories" to develop his "efficient incandescent lamp."

As Edison also said, "Genius is one percent inspiration and ninety-nine percent perspiration." Doing big things requires doing many, many insignificant or laborious things. By small things are great things brought to pass.

My granddad was big on acronyms. "KTYL!" he would say to departing loved ones. We understood what he was saying, "Know that you're loved." He had all kinds of acronyms and used them as a kind of code to communicate important ideas. The one I remember the most from him is PPPG: *persistence pays pretty good*. And after trying to apply this message from my grandfather in my own life for a couple decades, I've learned how powerful it is.

Many people wimp out when things get hard or when they first fail. It's easy to take the path of least resistance, obviously, instead of reading a lengthy book on a deep topic, why not play video games instead? But doing things that are fun and easy often means long-term failure in life; those who quit whenever they face problems never stick with something long enough to benefit from it. They deprive their future self of success. They seek short-term gratification over long-term greatness.

Persistence requires being patient with yourself. Good things are often hard, and hard things take time. Take a long view in your life and invest now in the difficult things that will lead to future success. Be persistent in pursuing your big goals. Remember: PPPG.

FIND A MENTOR

YOUR PARENTS LOVE YOU and want you to be successful and happy, but teenagers often develop a bit of a... shall we say...rebellious streak. It's sometimes hard to consider that everything our parents suggest is exactly what we should do. And honestly, parents don't have all the answers; we're often making it up as we go! That's why having access to a mentor can be so powerful; having another perspective from someone who also cares for you and wants you to succeed can give you additional guidance that's often extremely helpful to consider.

First, understand what the purpose of a mentor is. This person shouldn't tell you what to do or what life decisions to make. They should be a confidential listener who believes in you and helps you find your own answers, with their questions and ideas guiding you. And to make the most of it, you'll want to consider what your current goals are related to your education, friendships, interests, or career. What personal or learning challenges are you facing? Maybe you don't yet have ambitious goals, and that's okay. A mentor can help guide you to discover yourself a bit more.

So how do you find one? Make a list of adults you already know. It could be a teacher, neighbor, member of your church, friend of your parents, etc. Whom do you most admire, and why? Which of the people on your list might best support your goals?

Narrow down your list to a small handful and ask each of them for 30 minutes of their time to tell them you're looking for a mentor and what you would want out of it. Explain why you're asking them and why you think it would benefit you. (They'll be flattered, believe me.) Discuss your goals and challenges and ask if they'd be willing to meet with you once every other week to discuss and support your goals.

Once you've found someone who's willing and whom you want to build the relationship with, be open and honest in your discussions. Ask questions. Learn how they think. Commit to doing what they suggest and reporting back on how it went. Invest in this mentor process and you'll find some strong rewards to help you along your journey.

START A SIDE HUSTLE OR TWO

NEARLY HALF OF AMERICANS have a "side hustle," an extra job, freelance career, or small business they operate in addition to their full-time focus (whether that be a 9-to-5 job, raising kids, or going to school). There's no reason why you shouldn't be in this group.

All you need to get started is finding a problem people have. For 15-year-old Noa Mintz, it was the fact that her parents had struggled for years to find babysitters who would do more than just sit on their phone, disengaged from the kids they were supposed to interact with. So, she started "Nannies by Noa," a company that pairs families with highly engaged caretakers whom she personally vets. Families love having the help in identifying quality babysitters (or more regular nannies) and pay her a finder's fee and a portion of every payment. Things grew so well that Noa, still in school, was able to hire a full-time CEO to take over operations and keep growing the company. "It's amazing to see what I'm capable of," she remarked. "I always say, 'Don't let my age get in the way.'"

Neither should you. And not every venture will succeed like Noa's did, but that's the beauty of experimentation. You learn even from the failures, and you apply that new knowledge to your next endeavor. You can start an e-commerce business, create a YouTube channel, find gigs on Fiverr or Upwork, transcribe documents, test or review video games, create websites, and so much more. There are endless opportunities for entrepreneurs. Why? Because people always have problems in life, and they need solutions. You can be a part of that.

What's great about doing this at your age is that young people rarely have "analysis paralysis," which leads people (typically adults) to avoid beginning something new before it's analyzed from multiple angles. Just go for it, even if you don't get it right the first time. And recognize that it's okay to ask questions to learn. Especially at your age, people will be ready and eager to help.

Treat your side hustle as a hobby that can make you money, eventually paying for itself and ideally growing into something that can create a better future for you and, maybe like Noa, for others you're able to employ and help along their own journey in life.

LEARN TO COMMUNICATE

IF YOU DON'T WANT to suck at life, then you'll need to be a great communicator. I'm not talking about being able to stand up on stage and dazzle audiences with your intellect, though gaining that skill is certainly helpful. I mean one-on-one-conversations when you resolve conflict with someone, persuade someone, build a relationship, and help others or are helped by them.

These intimate and deep connections will most help you in life, so it's critical that you learn how to communicate well with family, friends, classmates, colleagues, and others. First, recognize that this requires an investment of time. Instead of shrugging off a question you're asked or giving the briefest answer possible, take time to elaborate and engage. Reciprocate by asking a question of the other person, which shows you care. And really listen; spend the mental energy to focus on what the other person says and means, which is one of the most engaging things you can do in a conversation. Don't try to cut things short so you can move on with your day or return to scrolling on your phone. Be willing to connect and spend the time that that requires.

Body language is a significant part of communication, which is why connecting with others in person is so important. I remember once in the early 2000s when I broke up with my girlfriend in a text. That didn't end well (shocking, I know) because it didn't allow her to understand what I actually felt and thought. It didn't give her an opportunity to react and resolve the tension. Emojis, while helpful, don't smooth over plain text enough to make it worth it. Be brave enough (like I apparently wasn't) to have difficult conversations and share how you feel with others.

Be clear and direct. Say what you feel and get to the point. Don't beat around the bush or use passive language. And want to know a real sign of maturity? Be willing to admit when you're wrong, apologize, and resolve a problem by moving forward, committed to improvement. Most adults lack many of these skills. Don't be among that group.

18-YEAR-OLDS AREN'T ADULTS

TEENAGERS HAVE LONG DONE many "adult" things. At the age of 16, Alexander the Great was already conquering other people; Joan of Arc, at the same age, was already bossing around military officers and demanding an audience with the king. Julius Caesar was already head of his family at 16. And, of course, most of the stories of teen greatness aren't told because they were so common. With youth managing farms, leading their families across the plains, starting families of their own, working their own land, and more. Maturity often came earlier in the past.

Today, adulthood is legally conferred at age 18. Poof! 6,570 days have passed since your birth, and now you're an adult. (At least, according to the government.) But children today have often been deprived of opportunities to work hard and embrace personal responsibility that would best prepare them for a life of independence. (Psst... another reason why being a free-range kid is crucial.)

The brains of teenagers aren't yet fully developed. The frontal lobe of the human brain is responsible for decision making, critical thinking, and rational thought; that's why teenagers often act impulsively and react emotionally. This area of the brain doesn't fully develop until one's mid-20s, and even potentially close to hitting age 30, long after the age when most cultures in the world consider you an adult.

So, what's magic about the age of 18? Nothing. Younger people have matured more quickly by having to take on additional responsibility, due to the death of parents or similar circumstances. And there are plenty of "adults" in their 20s or 30s who still act and think like teenagers, deprived of the experiences that would help them mature.

All of this is to say, don't expect life to suddenly change when you're 18. Take on responsibility now that will better prepare you for actual adulthood. Don't be a 20-something basement dweller who still relies on your parents for basic needs. Instead of waiting for the world to change when you've been alive for 6,570 days, start making changes now.

SEE WHAT IS UNSEEN

"THAT'S JUST THE TIP of the iceberg" is a common saying that's actually pretty significant, but rarely applied. It refers to a situation when you learn something that's actually a small part of something much larger that you should also be aware of. The saying makes sense because an iceberg's visible portion is typically quite small compared to the massive area underneath the water, out of view. Navigating iceberg-filled waters requires seeing what's unseen.

The problem? Most people only focus on what they can see. When I was a teenager, a raging fire spread throughout my community, destroying dozens of homes. Predictably, the local news stations were interviewing all kinds of "experts" about the situation, including an economist from the local university, who reassured viewers that the fires were actually a good thing.

Wait, what? I was stunned. But he was adamant in his view, claiming that the destroyed homes would create jobs for construction workers and all the people involved in the supply chain, which ultimately was a good thing for the economy. This made no sense, yet here this guy was championing destruction as a positive thing because it requires rebuilding.

As I later learned, this is the sign of a really bad economist, someone who focuses on what's seen, and reacts to it narrowly, just as with a ship captain only paying attention to the tip of the iceberg. A good economist also focuses on things that are unseen. In the case of the fire, that would be all the ways that money could have been used instead. People could have bought cars, had babies, created a garden, started companies, etc., all while still having homes as well.

I've since realized that humans are really good at ignoring things they can't see. They often have tunnel vision and focus on what's in front of them. They rarely contemplate factors and influences that aren't immediately apparent but that are still important. Want to be wise? Then try to see what's unseen. Take more into consideration than what's easily in front of you. Ask questions and dig deeper. Figure out the real size of the iceberg before navigating ahead in life.

PRISONS AND SCHOOLS ARE SIMILAR

RANDALL LEE CHURCH WAS sentenced to prison in 1983 for fatally stabbing a man. Released in 2011, he couldn't adjust to a totally changed world that had moved on without him. "Everything had gone fast forward without me," he said in an interview. Just 3 months of freedom was enough to convince him that he couldn't handle it. He wanted to go back to prison.

Church burned down a house to make it happen.

Not every released convict wants to return to prison, but many struggle with their newfound freedom. "There are a lot of people who do not want to go back to jail," said one prison chaplain. "They want to do the right thing, but they don't know how. They don't know how to be free people. In prison you learn life values that are useless in the real world."

It must be an odd experience to abruptly switch from imprisonment to freedom. Yet this is precisely what happens at the conclusion of one's time in the modern schooling system, where millions of teenagers graduate and wonder what to do next.

They, too, have learned information that's "useless in the real world" and struggle to succeed.

The comparison between school and prison is, sadly, a valid one. In both institutions, the subjects must navigate an authoritarian system: emphasis is placed on obedience and order; a dress code must be followed; individual autonomy is largely prohibited; schedules are micro-managed; permission is required to use the restroom; no input is allowed for any decision making; and those who break a rule are swiftly punished. Students and prisoners alike are rewarded for "good" behavior, conditioning them to do what they're told, rather than what they desire. Individual identity is diminished.

But prisoners can prepare for their next phase of life, despite whatever restrictions they're under. They can seek meaningful education and learn skills that will help them be self-sufficient. They can develop good character and come up with a plan. The same goes for high school students. Don't let the system prevent you from succeeding, and don't assume that good grades and graduation are enough.

LEARN TO FORGIVE

IF IT HASN'T HAPPENED already, at some point in your life, you'll be wronged by someone else. People do stupid things, and some people do horrible things. You'll be in the crosshairs at some point, subjected to someone's statement, decision, or action that hurts you, whether physically, emotionally, financially, or otherwise. Troubles such as these are simply part of a life filled with other people who do things differently than you.

But these "wrongs" are typically transitory, and life moves on; time heals most wounds. The problem comes when you hang onto your negative feelings about these incidents and let them fester. In this sense, you become your own worst enemy, as you inflict self-pain that prevents you from moving forward long after the wrong occurred.

I was bullied a lot in high school. I was a year ahead for my age and a late bloomer. Those two factors combined to create an awful experience. I looked like I was in 7th grade, making easy prey for the senior predators roaming the hallway. I was stuffed into trash cans, called all kinds of names, shoved around, teased, and plenty more. I hated it, and I was very angry. I felt worthless and didn't like my body. It wasn't a pleasant experience, and you couldn't pay me enough to relive those years.

But I hung onto these emotions long after I hit puberty. I remained insecure about my appearance and lacked confidence around others. I was distrustful and still angry. At whom, I couldn't say. I was just angry.

I finally let go of these emotions and decided to forgive those who had bullied me. After all, they were just kids, too. Kids do stupid things. It was time to move on. And I forgave myself for handling these issues poorly. I chalked it up to a learning opportunity and decided to think differently.

It's a process, but a critical one: you must learn to forgive those who wrong you and forgive yourself when you do something wrong. Life is about learning and growth, and we're all imperfect people. Be willing to move past the past and look to the future, free from the emotional baggage that will weigh you down from reaching greater heights.

STUDY THE HUMAN MIND

A PERSON IS SMART, but people are often stupid.

Plenty of research substantiates this point. Over and over again, people conform to the crowd and suppress their own rational thinking in order to do what others are doing; we pursue a shortcut in our brain by assuming that if others are doing it, then it must be right. This spares us the effort of doing the thinking ourselves. Studies show that people frequently adopt the view of the majority even when it's obviously wrong, and even if they have to deny their very own senses. Crazy, right? But it happens, over and over again.

There are two reasons why studying the human mind will help you in light of these troubling findings. The first is that you can better defend yourself against such trends. You don't want to be swept up into the stupid majority and let peer pressure dictate your decisions, so you need to be able to understand how and why groups of people operate the way they do. You can't avoid a problem you don't understand, which is why learning about psychology (the study of the human mind) is so helpful.

The second reason you need to learn about this is so that you can be influential in persuading others, in whatever career or life path you choose. Maybe you'll need to sell something, win over converts, find supporters, cultivate donors, or get neighbors to vote down a tax referendum. Put simply, life is full of opportunities to succeed by persuading other people. If you can get the crowd to support your position, you'll succeed.

This knowledge is a dangerous tool that needs to be used properly. Want to know how the tool can be abused? Read *Propaganda* by Edward Bernays. Curious how it can be used in a good way? Check out *Influence* by Robert Cialdini. And to really get to the heart of the matter, spend some time reading *The Crowd* by Gustave Le Bon. These books will make you realize how dangerous groups of people can be, and why you need to study enough to stand your ground against these powerful psychological currents.

VALUE LIBERTY, NOT SECURITY

IMAGINE STANDING UP TO the biggest superpower in the world with a measly military, basically farmers with rifles. That's what the colonists in America did, and we know how the story ended. But looking back on the revolutionary events, Thomas Jefferson observed that many people "prefer the calm of despotism to the tempestuous sea of liberty." Freedom is dangerous, unpredictable, and sometimes abused by those who have it. That's why many seem to prefer the "calm of despotism," a centrally planned life in which a few deciders get to dictate how we should behave in order to create conformity that makes people feel comfortable.

Why do people prefer despotism? That sounds crazy, right? The answer lies in the fact that despotism is always cloaked in the promise of security. People don't surrender their rights because they want a dictator to boss them around. What they want is to feel safe, physically and financially. And despots promise these things in order to gain power, even though they can't deliver. As

Benjamin Franklin once said, those who give up liberty to obtain temporary safety deserve neither liberty nor safety (and will likely have neither).

We see this all around us. After 9/11, people got scared and wanted to feel safe, so now we have (among many other things) the TSA at airports that rifles through our bags, pats down our bodies, uses technology to see through our clothes, and more. (This despite the fact that the agency consistently fails audits which test whether they actually find weapons.) Covid-19 happened, and we were faced with lockdowns and mandates, including being prohibited from going to church or gathering as families in some cases.

It's easy to be scared when there's a threat, especially one that's little understood. When we lack information, we're more likely to be afraid. That's why critical thinking and doing research is so important; by seeking to understand the truth, you'll have more confidence and knowledge and then better resist the despots who want to scare you into supporting them (and growing government). Value liberty over security and be on guard for anyone who wants you to surrender your freedoms for feelings of safety. Curious to learn more about this? Check out my book *Feardom*.

WHAT'S WORTHWHILE
IS HARD

I REALLY DON'T LIKE going to the gym, but I like being strong. Writing a book (ahem...) takes a really long time, but I like having a finished book I can share with others. Weeding my yard is tedious and repetitive, but I like having everything look nice. You catch my drift.

People often think that success looks like a straight line in an upward trajectory, a steady slope of activity that leads you from point A to point B. But success is messy, and that line is full of zigs and zags, loops in circles, and ups and downs before you (hopefully) arrive at point B. And if you were to stretch that messy line to be perfectly straight, it would be really long, far longer than the theoretical straight line between the two points.

Ever climbed a mountain? Most of your time is spent on the mountainside, putting one step in front of the other in pursuit of your goal. And when you finally summit the peak, what happens? You soak in the view, spend some time looking around, but then you move on. You start thinking of what mountain you'll climb next... not because you want another 30 minutes of a nice view—let's be honest, we have VR headsets, YouTube, and other things to satisfy those needs—but because you enjoyed and benefitted from the process. You increased your confidence, strengthened your body, and cleared your mind. The process was as important, or perhaps more so, than arriving at the destination.

Theodore Roosevelt said, well over a century ago, "The best prize that life offers is the chance to work hard at work worth doing." Ask your grandparents about the value of hard work, and they'll unleash stories upon you that will reinforce this point. It's the resistance that helps us succeed the most; muscles don't grow without it, and neither do our brains. You'll soon discover, if you haven't yet, that we learn more from what went wrong than what went right. Challenge leads to innovation; struggle inspires change. So, embrace the hard things in life, because you'll later learn they were typically the most worthwhile and helped you the most.

CHOOSE YOUR CRITICS CAREFULLY

SINCE YOU'RE READING THIS book, then you're the type of person who wants to improve. You want to make yourself better and the world as well. As you grow older, you'll launch projects, maybe start a business, do innovative things, stand up for what's right, and speak out in defense of truth. You're learning to become a leader, which means you're willing to take a few steps ahead into the darkness of uncertainty, while others are content to follow folks like you once the path is clearer.

Since you're an imperfect human, you'll inevitably make mistakes as you move forward in life, and your mistakes might impact others who are working with or for you. And even when you don't make mistakes, plenty of people will have differing opinions and think that you should have done something differently than whatever you decided. All of this is to say, you'll have critics aplenty; people will be surprisingly eager to vocalize their displeasure with whatever you did. This was not something I was prepared for.

I've been involved in changing a bunch of laws in the past several years and have fought hard to limit the government's power. That's what we do at Libertas Institute, but leading out on all kinds of political battles means that we come into conflict with those who disagree. And social media gives everyone a platform, making it easy for them to criticize me, make accusations against me, and even make fun of me. It happens daily, and I've had to develop some pretty thick skin.

So, what do I do? More importantly, what should you do? My advice is simple: don't take criticism from someone you wouldn't take advice from. Think that over for a second. Plenty of people will want to tear you down out of spite, or jealousy, or who knows what. Those critics don't have your best interests at heart and couldn't care less if you succeed. But there are people who love and support you who will critique your efforts with the goal of helping you improve. Focus on these voices and take to heart the feedback they give. In a world full of opinions and criticisms swirling on social media and elsewhere, choose your critics carefully and only pay heed to those who wish you well.

BE A GOOD FRIEND

WE ALL KNOW THE Golden Rule. It's easy to repeat, and it's something we understand to be a basic rule for being a decent human. We should treat others the way that we want to be treated by them. Sounds smart, right?

Of course, it's hard to put into practice because of its proactive nature. It doesn't mean that we should just be nice to those who reach out to us. It's not a rule for how we should respond to those who impact us in some way. Rather, it's a rule that requires us to actually do good things for other people, since we obviously want others to do good things for us. It asks us to make an investment, of our time, our energy, even our emotion, in other people, with the hope that this investment will generate returns of similar good things heading our way.

Think of your best friends who have supported you the most. They attend your sports games, suggest fun activities to do together, buy you something they think you'd like, compliment you, ask you questions and genuinely listen, and spend time with you when they could surely be doing something else. They put in effort to be a part of your life and show clear interest in you. You feel good about this; who wouldn't?

What kind of friend are you to others? And while it's easy to be friendly to a core few people, how do you behave towards others who aren't already your closest friends? Do you say hello to the new kid in the neighborhood and invite them to do something? How do you behave around the loner or outcast? Being a good friend doesn't always even require spending a lot of time with someone. Simply being friendly and supportive is enough to let the other person know you actually care. This can make a world of different to another person, especially if they're going through a tough time.

Don't just know about the Golden Rule; try to put it into practice and see how the experiment works for you. Be a good friend to others, and you'll find that you'll have more friends doing more things for you when you need it most.

DON'T HURT PEOPLE AND DON'T TAKE THEIR STUFF

I'VE NOTICED AN INTERESTING trend as I've become more involved politically: everyone is pretty libertarian when it comes to their own property and what they want. People want the freedom to do what they want in the way they want to do it. The problem is that few of these same people are willing to allow others that same desire; most people want to be free but want to control others. For example, someone might gripe about the taxes they have to pay, but then vote for a tax increase for a new park since they want to use it for their kids, without thinking or caring that they're forcing other people who don't care about a park to pay for it. This inconsistency is common.

Democracy is mob rule, the "tyranny of the majority." Yet so many people think they should be able to use the law to get their way on whatever the issue is and impose that desire on the dissenting minority, forcing them to go along with it. You'll see it over and over again as you get older: people asking the government to do things for them, which forces other people to pay for and support whatever it is. You'll be on the minority end of things often, no doubt, which makes this process especially painful.

Ultimately, true laws rest on this simple foundation: don't hurt people and don't take their stuff. Life, liberty, and property are basic rights deserving of protection, and people (including the government!) should be prohibited from harming innocent people or taking their property. But so-called "laws" violate these basic principles all the time, sadly. That's why it's essential to understand what true laws are because you can't stick up for your rights if you don't first understand them. The easiest way to start is to read *The Law* by Frédéric Bastiat, an essay that packs a punch in helping readers understand these ideas. (Your younger siblings should check out *The Tuttle Twins Learn About the Law*, a version for kids!)

THE GOOD GUY DOESN'T ALWAYS WIN

THE "HERO'S JOURNEY" IS a formulaic approach to the epic novels and movies we all know and love. It goes like this: a reluctant hero is called to an adventure in a strange land, and with the help of a guide discovers a new power or item to help him, uses it to defeat a villain, then returns home victorious. It's seen in The Lion the Witch and the Wardrobe, The Matrix, Lord of the Rings, Harry Potter, Star Wars, Men in Black, Alice in Wonderland, and many more stories.

It's great to celebrate the hero's victory, but perhaps there's a reason why these stories are fictional; in the real world, the would-be hero often fails to accomplish their objective. Not all adventures result in success against all odds. The odds often are stacked against the good guy and ends the adventure before it has a chance to begin.

Of course, this happens all the time; corrupt politicians win elections, unethical business owners prosper, mean kids are popular, immoral individuals are praised, etc. But that doesn't take away the sting of defeat. I was a vocal supporter of Ron Paul during his presidential campaigns. I had hope that he stood a chance, especially in the 2008 election. But the media suppressed him, gave much more air time to his less-popular competitors, and tried their hardest to ignore him so his message couldn't get out. He ultimately lost the Republican nomination, and I was upset. The good guy had lost.

But had Ron Paul not put himself out there, despite losing, I would not have learned about liberty or read the books he recommended. Chances are I wouldn't have started my successful think tank Libertas Institute which has benefitted hundreds of thousands of people with the laws we have changed, nor would my friend Elijah and I have started the *Tuttle Twins*, which have educated and helped millions. Good guys may not win, but that doesn't mean we shouldn't still be good and let our influence impact others in whatever way possible. Stand up for what's right, even if those choosing wrong have a temporary victory.

DON'T BE WOKE

IN EARLY 2021, A whistleblower released screenshots of a "diversity training" that Coca-Cola was making its employees sit through, which urged them to "Be less white." These silly examples of woke-ness are seemingly everywhere: renaming schools that once bore the names of people who are now deemed to be insufficiently righteous; students demanding that supposedly "white supremacist" European books be replaced with non-European reading materials; people being slammed for "cultural appropriation" for wearing outfits or eating meals typically found among cultures they aren't ethnically a part of; and telling basically everyone to "check their privilege" and debase themselves.

Woke-ness is fundamentally about being caught up in the chaotic cultural tides of political correctness, only saying or doing what mob mentality has agreed is proper. It fights those who stand firm on a foundation of truth and principle, since solid positions are a threat to its fluid nature. The woke crowd detests those who affirm that objective truth exists. They hate those who will not apologize for their own existence and heritage. How dare you be born to a "privileged" family in a "capitalist" country with whatever amount of "whiteness" you have that's a threat to "inclusivity!"

There's a broader point here, and it's one most kids are taught at a younger age: don't succumb to peer pressure. Sure, the message applies to drugs and sex and such things, but it applies equally to sociocultural trends, too. When those around you are regurgitating the new slogans and statements they learned on the latest social media app, it's generally a good idea to avoid their new nonsense and remain focused on foundational truths and principles that lead to human happiness and well-being. Reject the ever-changing demands of the mob and pay them no heed; people, after all, become pretty dumb in large groups. Truth is better found through individual study than following the herd's wandering ways.

I don't know a single "woke" person who is happy. They seem fueled by anger, always complaining about some perceived injustice. You're a free-thinking person, so act like it. Be anti-woke.

BUILD A NETWORK

WHOM DO YOU HANG out with? Whom do you spend most of your free time with? What kind of influence do these people have on you? Do they build you up to be a better person? Do they inspire you? Are they the type of people you want to become? Looking back on your life 20 years from now, will you consider these relationships beneficial?

There's an important lesson you should learn and apply immediately, shared by Jim Rohn, a motivational speaker: "You are the average of the five people you spend the most time with." This seems self-evident, right? The people who you spend your time with will shape who you become. They influence the conversations and ideas that capture your attention. They deeply affect your attitude and emotions, even your behaviors. To a large degree, you'll start to think like they think and behave like they behave.

It may seem self-evident to you, but chances are that you're like almost everyone else; you're passive about this reality. You don't actively seek to shape your environment, creating or ending friendships with a goal of creating a network of people around you who will inspire and influence you to become better. But this is critical because, as one researcher found, the people you regularly associate with "determine as much as 95 percent of your success or failure in life."

Your environment, the people who are a part of your life, plays a significant role in determining who you'll become. So why not recognize that reality and actively construct your environment in order to increase your chances of personal and professional success? Don't let chance or proximity (those who happen to live in your neighborhood) decide this for you. Decide what types of opinions, attitudes, and perspectives you do and do not want to be in your life and pursue your friendships and relationships accordingly.

If you're the product of the people around you, then you need to build a network of people who are what you want to become. Mentors, entrepreneurs, ambitious individuals, people with positive energy... choose wisely, and be intentional about whom you let into your life.

GO TO ORIGINAL SOURCES

EVER PLAYED THAT "TELEPHONE" game, where one person starts a message and it ends up totally different at the end? People are connected in a line, and one person relays the message to the next person and so on, until the end where the message has become corrupted, sometimes intentionally, often inadvertently. Either way, the accurate information is lost.

I once read an article written on someone's blog, a report about a meeting that had happened at the Capitol. But the blogger wasn't at the meeting. The source of their information was someone who had posted on Twitter about the meeting. But that person wasn't there either; their source was a newspaper article, written by a journalist who was there. I laughed, seeing a telephone game play out right in front of me.

But that's not the worst of it. I've been in a lot of meetings where reporters attempt to summarize for the public what happened. Then I read the write-up of what they claimed happen, and I always roll my eyes because it's maybe 2% of what actually was said and done. And the parts that are summarized are often slanted or clearly biased. I lament how uninformed the public is if they rely on the "telephone" provided by the media, which is ineffective, even though it's not a long chain of people repeating information.

This is why going to original sources is so critical in your research about history, current events, or whatever truth you seek. People are blown away when I share details about these meetings I'm a part of because they recognize how little they actually know about what is going on. Reading the Declaration of Independence is better than reading a textbook's summary about it. Listening to a researcher on a podcast interview is better than reading an article about the researcher. Go deeper, find the sources of the information who know deeply about what's going on, and gain direct insights that will make you more informed and aware than simply relying on telephone-like summaries that are often incomplete and inaccurate. The truth is out there, but you have to go digging for it a bit.

CHALLENGE TRADITION

"WHY DID YOU GET rid of that much ham?" a stunned husband asked his wife, seeing her cut off a chunk and throw it away as she prepared to put the rest in the oven.

"That's the way I've always done it," she replied. "It's how my mom taught me to do it."

Thinking this was really odd, the man called his mother-in-law to verify his wife's story and learn why she had taught her to cut off so much ham.

"I've done it that way my whole life," she explained. "It's how I learned to do it from my mother."

The perplexed husband couldn't let this go, so at the next family gathering, when his wife's elderly grandmother was there, he approached her to ask about the ham story. She shrugged and held out her hands about nine inches apart.

"I had to cut it off to fit the rest in the only pan I had," she answered.

This fictional story, albeit a silly example, shows the dangers of tradition, the problems that come when we rely on doing things the way we've been told to do them by those who came before.

Showing a preference for the status quo is convenient, of course. After all, who wants to take the time to learn something new, or worse, discover that you've been doing something wrong, or even bad, for your whole life? It can be uncomfortable to challenge tradition.

But challenge tradition you must because there are plenty of ideas, attitudes, beliefs, and practices that are misinformed, wrong, or even harmful. Even if they're well-intentioned, it's best that you regularly examine why you believe and do what you do to ensure that your time and energy are being put to best use. Every step you take up a ladder that's against the wrong building takes you in a direction you shouldn't be going. Make sure, then, that your ladder is resting against the right wall.

PLAY AN INSTRUMENT

IF YOU'RE LIKE ME, your parents made you practice the piano growing up. I really didn't like it, and I struggled. But they insisted I had to muddle through it, so I did it. But it didn't stick. I was finally allowed to decide for myself, and I decided to quit. I soon lost whatever skills I had developed, and now I can't play at all. But I really loved the saxophone. I was in several bands with friends as a teenager, which was an amazing experience. I picked up the guitar a bit, and two decades later I'm learning how to play the drums. These creative outlets have been an enjoyable part of my life.

As it turns out, there are dozens of benefits from learning an instrument. Perhaps an obvious one is that the practicing required to develop a certain level of mastery helps you develop patience and discipline. It creates focus by helping you achieve a large goal (mastery) through a steady series of bite-sized micro-goals (daily practice). The confidence boost you get (and the dopamine rush your brain is given) is yet another aspect that has application to other areas of your life.

Learning to create music obviously cultivates creativity, by strengthening those areas of your brain. Because playing an instrument engages the entire brain, it actually increases blood circulation and stimulates connections throughout, helping increase your performance in other areas of life. Want to be smart, think clearly, and have a sharp wit? There are few things as helpful as creating music.

There are so many more benefits: it improves your memory retention, helps you develop social skills, regulates emotional well-being, relieves stress, improves motor and coordination skills, teaches teamwork, cultivates risk-taking, and on and on. It's one thing to want to jam with some friends and create music. Believe me; that's a thrill worth being a part of, if for nothing else than the memories you'll create along the way. But your life will be improved in so many ways through music that it just makes sense to pick your preferred instrument and start practicing!

FINISH WHAT YOU START

THE GUITAR I'VE LONG wanted to learn how to play sits idle, gathering dust in the corner of my office, taunting me. I've started several times but haven't dedicated the time necessary to finish. I'm nowhere near the point of mastery. This guitar has become a reminder for me to finish what I start or, perhaps, not start things unless I have the time and desire to see it through.

Think of the great innovators of world history. Take Johannes Gutenberg, for example, who created the first printing press with movable type. This was a remarkable revolution in communication, but it didn't happen overnight. Through persistence and overcoming failure, Gutenberg finished what he started, and the result was transformational. Imagine what the world would be like today had he become distracted from his project or resigned to defeat after one of his early struggles during the process of refining his idea.

You gain power from crossing the finish line. But what prevents you from getting there? Perhaps the greatest obstacle is you: your fears, anxieties, and self-doubt. Maybe you just lack focus and don't prioritize your time well. These factors should be faced directly; you need to analyze yourself, identify your weaknesses, and create a plan for how you can still progress in spite of them. The longer we delay, the more we deprive ourselves of learning opportunities that can help us move forward.

Do you want to be the type of person who finishes what they begin and follows through on what they intend? Or will you settle for being someone who's always half done, meandering through the middle, never consistently moving forward? Whatever the project is, sometimes, the best option is to simply get to the end, so you can check it off your list, consider it "done," and feel the sense of accomplishment that comes from completion.

But recognize that no matter how much you accomplish, you'll always have a few things that get de-prioritized; you'll have your own dusty guitars nagging at you. And that's okay; with a finite amount of time in life, not every finish line is worth pursuing.

PLAN YOUR FUNERAL

I'M THE TYPE OF person who wants to make a difference. I want to make a lasting impact on others and change the world. I want to help those around me on their journey and share what I've been able to acquire and learn. And I think about these things a lot because life is short.

Life may not seem short when you're young, but ask your parents or grandparents; their lives are flying by. Time moves faster as you get older, and you start running out. And death can come at any time. Who knows? Could be tomorrow. So... what do you want people to know and remember you for?

I remember attending a funeral for someone who was... shall we say, average? He didn't appear to have many strong relationships, left a somewhat checkered past, and people clearly struggled to find nice things to say. So, they spoke in generalities. I wondered to myself: does anyone care that this guy is gone? Did his life matter? Who did it matter to, and why? It led me to start thinking about what I want people to say about me when I'm gone. A hundred years from now, do I want people to remember me? What stories do I want my grandchildren to remember and share about me with their own kids?

It turns out that thinking about what you want others to say about your funeral is a great way to align your life now in a direction that will lead to those remarks. And it's not like you want to give these people a script to read; you want them to authentically remember you as a loving person, someone who brought them joy, someone who helped them, someone who's work made a difference to change others' lives, etc. And if you want them to believe and share those feelings, you have to work now to be that type of person.

You have your whole life ahead of you, but one day, a summary of that life will be written. You should start thinking now about what you want it to say.

DON'T TAKE YOURSELF TOO SERIOUSLY

THERE'S A LOT IN this book that will help you improve your life. But there's also a risk with coming up with all these suggestions for you: you might take yourself too seriously. Note the *too*. It's important to be serious (intentional, focused, studious, persistent, etc.) about your efforts to grow and build and progress. But there's a fine line you need to be aware of, a balance you need to achieve, that offsets this intensity with some lightheartedness.

Life is going to get more complex for you in the years ahead. You'll worry about relationship problems, stress from work, bills to pay, obligations to discharge, family drama, and on and on. These will all need to be dealt with, to be sure. But there's something to be said for cultivating a sense of playfulness about your life. You can't always control what happens to you, but you can control how you react.

Let me use an example. Imagine you're in a group setting and someone makes a joke at your expense in front of others. You get red in the face, upset with the jokester, and resentful about feeling a bit outcast from the group. But now consider a different approach where you're the first person to laugh. It's disarming! This levity would show that you understand you may have flaws and you're not afraid if others recognize that. You can brush it off. Laughing at yourself is an important step to recognizing that not everything is the end of the world; some things just aren't worth taking seriously.

Look, you're not perfect. You're going to make mistakes and do things wrong. We all do. So, learn to joke about the things that you're sensitive to; embrace them and laugh at them. Do you cry while watching Disney movies? Own up to it and be silly about it. Maybe you get really gassy after eating your mom's chili. Lean into it and joke it up. It'll loosen you up and make you less worried about what others think about you. It might seem counterintuitive, but those who don't take themselves too seriously have a higher level of confidence that creates a certain strength in their life.

DON'T BE A CRAB
IN A BUCKET

DO YOU KNOW WHAT happens when you pile a bunch of crabs in a bucket? They stay there. The weird thing is that one of them can easily get out (provided you fill the bucket to the right height). It's possible. But it doesn't happen. Why? Because the other crabs prevent it from happening. As one crab starts to stretch upwards toward freedom, other crabs will pull it down.

It's crazy, but it doesn't just happen with crabs. Humans sometimes share a similar tendency by working against the interests of those around them. Jealousy, envy, and sometimes simple spite leads some people to tear down the efforts of others who are moving forward in life. These people seem to think in their minds, *If I can't get it, neither can you.* The world is full of these people. Perhaps you know someone like this. They might even be among your friends or family!

These "crabby" people think that life is a zero-sum game. Think of this like a pie we all get to share. If I take a few slices, then less that's available to you. It's in the other person's best interest to fight for as much of the pie as they can get before it's gone. If I get a lot, they get little. The problem with this way of thinking is that life is not a zero-sum game at all. If I make a bunch of money, that doesn't mean that you can't as well. If I sell a bunch of books, it doesn't prevent you from doing the same. If you achieve some special feat, I'm not prevented from doing that, too.

Cheer on the success of others. Support people when they do great things. Find a way to be genuinely happy for those you know when they excel at something. You'll be happier, you'll have stronger relationships, and, chances are, you could learn something from them that will help you attain similar results. If crabs were really smart, they'd let one another escape so that each crab could help the one behind. Be smarter than crabs.

WHO NOT HOW

YOU CAN'T DO EVERYTHING by yourself.

I've learned this the hard way. You see, I'm good at a lot of things, so, over time, I've just continued to do things myself and learn whatever else I need to know to accomplish my goals. That was fine up until a certain point, but then it became a limiting factor in my success. I became my own bottleneck.

I'll give you a specific example. I used to be a web developer, making websites and apps for a living. My political and educational work with Libertas Institute is quite different, yet, over the years, we've needed a variety of websites. So, I've created them. But then we need more and more, and I have less time than I used to. I finally had to realize that it would be better to pay someone else to do this for me, even though I could do it myself. My time was more valuable and better spent, doing other higher-level tasks.

It finally clicked for me when I read *Who Not How* by Dan Sullivan and Benjamin Hardy, which addressed this exact issue. The key to growth comes not by learning how to do all kinds of things, but by creating a network of people, a group of "whos," that surround you and can help you. Others who have expertise can get something done for you more quickly and cost-effectively than you can by spending all kinds of time trying to figure it out for yourself.

This is important because time is your most scarce resource. It burns up quickly and you can't get it back. So, instead of me spending hours figuring out how to repair my car, I take it to the mechanic who can do it better and more quickly. And while they're doing their thing, I do mine: I work on my laptop creating value for other people, which provides me the revenue I need to pay the mechanic. I focus on who I am, what my unique abilities are, and employ other "whos" to serve me in areas that I shouldn't spend my time on.

You don't need to learn and be and do everything. Don't focus on all the "hows" to become skilled in so many things. Focus on your strengths, and for all other areas, find a "who" to help.

THINK BEFORE ACTING

THIS ONE SEEMS OBVIOUS, right? It's the old adage, "Look before you leap." But no matter how many times we hear people say it, it doesn't always sink in.

When I was 16, I drove my parent's minivan to a party to hang out with friends. It was a warm summer day, and people were hanging out in the house and all around the driveway and street. When it came time for me to leave, a friend and I got in the car and I began to turn the ignition. Just then, another friend Amy hopped onto the hood of the car, her feet on the fender for support. She was laughing and messing around. Stupidly, I put my foot on the gas pedal and started to slowly drive forward. Laughs continued, which evidently egged me on a bit to suddenly accelerate the vehicle. Seeing the immediate shock on Amy's face prompted me to (stupidly) slam on the brakes, sending her skidding across the road. The aftermath wasn't pretty; she had severely torn up skin all over her legs and arms. You can imagine how I felt.

I was an idiot. I didn't think before I acted. I made an impulse decision without thinking through the consequences. Chances are, you do it as well. For example, you might indulge in a purchase of a video game system or trading cards or an expensive pair of shoes, perhaps in response to an advertisement you saw, a sale that created a sense of urgency, or a desire to have what others around you already have. But had you thought more about that decision, perhaps you would have decided to invest that money instead, using compound interest to generate "free" money for your future self.

Our actions have benefits and costs; we have to think through what we gain through a certain action, and what it costs us. Whether it's procrastinating chores, asking someone on a date, spending the weekend at the beach, going for a road trip, or working two jobs, our decisions have all kinds of consequences. Some may be trivial, and others may be life-threatening. Whatever the action is, we ought to be intentional in thinking about it first.

PEOPLE GIVE TO GIVERS

THE HARE KIRSHNA SOCIETY is a religious group that, for a long time, struggled to find ways to raise enough money for their operations. They acted and dressed differently, often in long robes, draped in beads and bells. Their efforts to solicit donations were often unsuccessful because people found them... well, weird. But then they switched their fundraising tactics and, instead, offered people gifts. These would typically be a book, a magazine, or even a simple flower. After giving their target person a gift, they would then ask for support. Things changed quickly, and the group started raising significant money through this strategy.

This fundraising tactic leverages what's known as the rule of reciprocity, a simple psychological behavior where people feel obligated to return a favor to someone if they feel indebted to them. It's almost as if our brains were wired to discharge debts and settle things between another person. If we feel we owe someone something, we actively seek opportunities to pay them back. We don't like owing other people things. This is why investing in others is key. By giving of your time, energy, or money to others, you're creating situations where these people will want to give back to you.

But becoming a giver is not just about the transactional relationships in which people to whom you give will directly want to give back to you. That's certainly a real thing, and you can leverage it to find mutually beneficial situations. Beyond that, though, there's something about being a giver that leads to broader opportunities outside of the people to whom you directly give. Givers are people whom others want to be around. They create bigger networks. They inevitably find that their giving has led, in indirect ways, to them finding abundance. They may not be getting things reciprocated from those to whom they give, but they find, repeatedly, that their charity and service and support of others leads to opportunities elsewhere that enrich them.

Be a giver. Help others. Give generously of your time and resources. You'll inevitably find that your giving gets you a lot in return.

MONITOR YOUR THOUGHTS

AS RALPH WALDO EMERSON once wrote, "You are what you think all day long." Our actions are the product of our thoughts. Our environment is shaped by what we think. We see the world in a way that's colored by our perspective. What we give voice to in our head becomes our reality.

So many people, especially young people, allow their minds to be flooded with negativity. They think they're not good enough, or too shy, or not good looking, or intimidated, or whatever. They let the fears bathe their brains and then limit their abilities because of what's in their own head. But what if you could be afraid and do the hard thing anyway? It's possible to have insecurities or concerns and still move forward.

Even better, what if you train your brain to engage in positive thinking? What if you try to manifest the better life you want, and state daily affirmations that empower rather than limit you? What if you programmed your mind to think that you're good enough, that you're confident, great looking, not intimidated, or whatever? Exercises as simple as daily affirmations can work wonders.

Why? Because you are exactly what you believe and think about. You are the creator of your own world, and if that world is full of obstacles you've put in front of yourself, then you'll never find a way forward. But if that world is painted in your mind as a limitless adventure that is filled with obstacles you can overcome, and find joy in the process of doing so, then you brain will literally rewire itself to empower you to take actions consistent with that way of thinking.

Especially with how prevalent mental health problems have become, you must monitor your thoughts and train your brain. Be intentional about positive thinking and make sure your mind is working for and with you, not against you.

KEEP A NOTEBOOK

SMART PEOPLE WRITE NOTES. It's that simple.

I was taught as a teenager that the best way to remember something is to write it down. Seems obvious, right? Turns out maybe that's not quite accurate. For example, in one study where people were asked to watch a lecture, half took notes and half didn't. But both groups remembered around 40% of the information covered in the lecture. So, was I taught wrong? Not really: the participants who had taken notes remembered a higher proportion of key facts, whereas those who didn't take notes remembered more of a random assortment of ideas from the lecture. In other words, those who took notes were focused on organizing the key information and later remembering what was most important.

What's happening in our brains when we take notes is that before we even write things down, we're putting some thought into evaluating and sorting the information we're hearing or thinking. It's that process, and not the notes themselves, that helps plant things in our minds more deeply, which leads to greater recall later. The note-taking process gives our mind an opportunity to focus more on what matters and remember it for the future. Taking good notes, then, often helps us remember things well enough that we don't even need our notes again.

This is why keeping a journal is also important because it gives our mind a space to process thoughts and seek clarity as we reflect on our day or week and organize what happened. We give conscious thought to things we otherwise wouldn't have focused on. We use the writing experience as a brain exercise to think and remember.

I used to prefer typing notes on my computer because I can do it faster. But one study suggests that writing by hand is more strongly linked to emotion processing compared to typing. Taking your time to write notes helps you think things over rather than just regurgitate them onto the screen. Again, it's not about the notes; it's about giving your brain an opportunity to think, sort, and remember.

CURATE YOUR DIGITAL PERSONA

YOUR PAST CAN HAUNT you. That's a hard lesson learned by many, including Alexi McCammond, an aspiring journalist. She landed a dream job, but soon found herself embroiled in controversy when a few problematic tweets she posted a decade prior, as a teenager, were found and reported. She apologized and clearly had matured as a young adult, but her employer caved into the rising pressure to fire her after advertisers started severing their ties with the publication. As her career got started, Alexi's legs were cut from under her by her own past self. She became a victim of the mob's unforgiving reaction to years-old content that was saved online.

Edward Snowden, the whistleblower who reported on the NSA's surveillance of the American people, wrote a book called *Permanent Record* in which he explained that because of modern technology, it was easy to build surveillance systems that are "a constant and indiscriminate presence: the ear that always hears, the eye that always sees, a memory that is sleepless and permanent." But it's not just the government spying on and collecting information about us. We willingly share all kinds of details and opinions, uploading them to the "cloud," to be saved on someone else's computer potentially forever.

There are significant ramifications to this, and young people rarely think about them, just as Alexi failed to forecast the career consequences her drive-by tweets would bring her in the years to come. For that reason, it's important to curate your digital persona now. This means being aware of what you say and share. Don't reveal things about yourself publicly that might be later used against you. Be cautious in how controversial or divisive you are and consider periodically scrubbing past social media content to prevent years-old irrelevant content from accumulating. After all, in a changing society, what was uncontroversial when you posted it may later become verboten and subject to scrutiny. Best be careful.

You have the power to shape others' perception about you, but you need to be intentional about this. Be judicious in what you post online, because of the potential permanence of what you say and do.

FAST

EARLY PHILOSOPHERS AND RELIGIOUS leaders alike all proclaimed the benefits of fasting for healing and spiritual rejuvenation. One of the fathers of Western medicine is claimed to have once said, "Fasting is the greatest remedy—the physician within."

Going without food for 24 hours (or up to 72 if you're super ambitious... which I'm not!) has all kinds of scientifically verified benefits that help you. And while these are interesting (reducing insulin resistance, fighting inflammation, boosting metabolism, and more) I believe that the power of fasting exceeds the physical realm. And this is perhaps why all major religions (Christianity, Judaism, Islam, Buddhism, Hinduism, and many more) incorporate fasting in their faith traditions. So, what is it about fasting that can help you?

Fasting is about more than just going without food. It's an opportunity for your spiritual self to master control over your physical self, mind over body. It helps us draw away from physical things, like our hunger, in order to have greater clarity of mind. And if you're religious, the process creates an opportunity where you can focus on God and aim to set aside, for a limited time, the constant physical demands of your mortal body. Sacrifice helps us show our commitment to a higher purpose or goal, and by going without food for a limited period of time, we can more deeply focus on what we desire or want to show gratitude for.

I believe success in life comes from living intentionally and learning to control our impulses in order to channel our energy in productive ways. Especially in our younger years, when our bodies are bathed in hormones and we act more impulsively, it's critical to temper any temptations and learn tactics that will help us focus and stay on a productive path in life. Fasting is one tool that can help us accomplish this by creating a sacrificial state in our life that requires us to think more deeply about what we have, what we want, and what we need to do to move forward in life.

DESIRE SOMETHING STRONGLY

I AM A DEEPLY dissatisfied person. The status quo, the current state of the world, troubles me.

For example, I'm a father of two kids. And when they were young, I was really bothered by the fact that there were no books to help me teach them the ideas of a free society. I was disappointed that someone else hadn't produced these resources. And as I reviewed the books being used in schools across the country, I was horrified at how awful they were, and how kids were being put through a system that dumbed down their education. This angst is what led me to start working on the Tuttle Twins books with my friend Elijah, our illustrator. (He shared my dissatisfaction with the status quo.) And now we've sold millions of these books to parents who see the same problem we did and want our help to solve it.

Here's the lesson: to achieve something great, you must have an intense desire. Look around at the world's most well-known-entrepreneurs and you're sure to find folks who have high levels of dissatisfaction. They're driven by this feeling to change it. They relentlessly pursue their goal because they're bothered by the status quo, whether it be inefficient delivery systems, the high cost of medicine, pollution from fossil-fuel vehicles, injustices in the government, etc. There are plenty of problems. You have to let one of them really, really bother you in order to have the motivation and energy to help solve it.

Flip this idea to see how true it is: people who have low levels of dissatisfaction are failures. They don't care about the problems around them because they don't feel impacted by them. They go with the flow and are content with the status quo. They're fine to live comfortably apathetic in the mainstream. They're good with "whatever."

If you want to be an achiever, you need to build an intense desire by focusing on and trying to fix whatever dissatisfies you. Make specific choices for the future about what you want to improve, and then refuse to be stopped by whatever obstacles stand in your way to make it a reality.

WRITE THANK YOU CARDS

I MEET A LOT of people because of my work; I regularly speak to large groups and have people coming up to me to introduce themselves, ask for help, or pitch me on an idea. When you do this for a while, it's easy to lose track of who's who; I struggle to remember names or where I know people from. But there are a small group of people who have buried themselves deeper in my mind; they're easier to remember. Why? Simply because they wrote me a thank you note.

Some of them have given it to me directly, others send it in the mail. But the experience is always so unique because it's rare. Few people do this. I suppose it's like that story in the Bible where Jesus healed ten lepers but only one ever returned to express his thanks. Whatever the reason, it's rare, and that's something you can leverage to your advantage.

You want to succeed in life. You want to build your network, create relationships in which you can serve and be served, and find those who can help you get ahead in life. Writing thank you cards to anyone who benefitted you is an extremely effective way to set yourself apart from others whom these people interact with. Perhaps it's a really good lecture from a professor, or a CEO who shared some insightful advice, or a coworker who did something nice for you, or a mentor whose support has helped you. Whatever it is, write a thank you card. Obviously, you shouldn't be doing this frequently for the same person, but when used appropriately, it will be seen for what it authentically is: a sincere gesture of gratitude that makes the recipient feel good.

In fact, I feel fantastic every time I get a thank you card. It helps me see the impact I'm having, and I'm honored to have helped the person who wrote it. It makes we want to help them even more! You can have that effect on others. All it takes is writing a few meaningful lines on a card where you share your thoughts and feelings for the other person.

PARTICIPATION TROPHIES ARE TRASH

I DON'T KNOW WHEN or why it started, but it's everywhere; sports teams are giving out awards, whether it's a trophy, a medal, or even a certificate, to each player, regardless of the outcome. These "participation trophies" might be an effort in inclusivity, but they're counterproductive. They hurt more than they help because when everyone wins, then everyone actually loses.

Young people need to be prepared for the real world, not coddled in some fantasy land of feel-goodery, wanting to keep their spirits up with unrealistic expectations. The raw fact of life is that not everyone wins; life isn't all sunshine and rainbows. Just because you have a college degree doesn't mean you'll get the job. Just because you swipe right on Tinder doesn't mean you'll get the girl or guy. Your bank account doesn't start adding Benjamins just because you exist. The human spirit is wired for overcoming, being resilient through failure and setbacks, applying ourselves to learn from mistakes, and then prevailing. That's what should get a trophy. We celebrate greatness, because it shows others what they can aspire to if they choose to work hard to attain it.

The real lesson here is that our society rewards laziness and losing; it subsidizes it and tries to lessen its impact. No job? Taxpayers will care for you. Made a bad decision? The government will bail you out. These bad ideas are the byproduct of a generation full of participant trophy recipients who feel entitled to progress and prosperity without having to work for it. In truth, it only leads to mediocrity, a path of least resistance that unproductive people follow to feel comfortable and cared for by others.

Reject the idea that you should be rewarded merely for participating in the process. Instead, learn how to master it. Trophies worth owning are those that recognize excellence. They inspire others to greatness and create an opportunity for those who don't earn them to learn how to lose with dignity but find pride in hard work and a determination to improve. Those are life lessons worth learning.

CONCLUSION

ARE YOU THE TYPE of person who reads a book cover to cover? Or perhaps you skimmed through this book focusing on the chapters that stood out to you. Whatever your approach, what's going to be most effective for you is considering these ideas on an ongoing basis. Why? Because you're quickly becoming a different person, experiencing new things, gaining new insights, and forming new perspectives. If you read this book again six months from now, there will be things you understand or appreciate differently than today.

What matters most, though, is forming an action plan. Start small. Pick two or three things from the book that you want to work on first—for example, writing thank you notes, journaling, and fasting. Decide how you'll go about it, and who can help hold you accountable to get it done. Create micro-goals to build up some momentum toward your bigger goals. Be intentional about it and be patient with yourself if it takes a bit of time.

We all have plenty of room for improvement, but if you take one thing away from this book, let it be this: life will improve if you're intentional about it. The opposite is also true because it's easy to suck at life and be a boring person who doesn't take risk or work hard. Sit back, let the world tell you what to think and do, and don't step outside your lane. Does that sound like the right formula for your future?

Each day is full of various decisions. You're in a constant state of change. You get to make yourself into whatever person you want to become. So right now, as you read these words, you get to make yet another choice: *will I do anything about what I've read? Is there something in my life I'll change? What am I going to do tomorrow with the information I read today?*

What type of person do I want to become?

It's your choice. Ready to get to work?

ABOUT THE AUTHOR

Connor Boyack is the founder and president of Libertas Institute, a free-market think tank in Utah. In that capacity, he has spearheaded a number of successful policy reforms in areas such as education reform, civil liberties, government transparency, business deregulation, personal freedom, and more. Several of these legal changes were the first of their kind in the country, and Libertas Institute has received numerous awards for their innovative work.

A public speaker and author of over 30 books, Connor is best known for *The Tuttle Twins* books, a children's series introducing young readers to economic, political, and civic principles.

Connor lives near Salt Lake City, Utah, with his wife and two homeschooled children.

Learn more at ConnorBoyack.com